embrace the imbalance

things you need to know from people i wish you knew

by tina mcintosh

This is a first-edition printing. It's special for a lot of reasons.

ISBN: 979-8-218-17713-3

Graphic designs: Maia McIntosh
Coaching & support: Emily Sutherland, www.emilysutherland.me

acknowledgments

My husband, Jeff ~ Thank you for allowing me to be the best version of myself and for living this life together. I would choose you again.

My oldest, Maia ~ You made me a mom. What a gift it has been to watch you come into this world and become the woman you are…exactly who God created you to be. Thank you for being such a special gift to so many people.

My son, Webster ~ Oh, Web. You are a smart, thoughtful, and charismatic young man. You probably don't realize the countless lessons you've taught me. I'm a better person because of you. It's an honor to be your mother.

My youngest, Georgia ~ You have been making me smile since the day you were born. Never stop being you, George, and your heart will be full. Thank you for showing me how great it is to be loved by someone like you.

My mom ~ I have every confidence that I am the person I am because you allowed me to make mistakes and learn from them and you rescued me when I needed rescuing. Thank you for teaching me so much along the way.

My dads ~ Yep. All three of you. Thank you, each of you, for the gifts each of you have instilled in me over the years.

My siblings ~ I love being your (considerably) older sister. Thank you for understanding that older means more experienced, but far from perfect. I am so impressed by who each of you has become as an adult.

My closest girlfriends ~ You know who you are. From the teen years, college years, single years, or getting-married-and-having-kids-years, to who we are right now, I cherish your friendships. And if I didn't write about you in this book, don't worry…there's still time.

My family & friends ~ I am so grateful that you choose to love me and that you share parts and pieces of your lives with me. I hope you always feel my love because it's always here.

Joy's House Guests, caregivers, staff, volunteers, donors & any other stakeholders ~ I can't possibly name you all, but you have shaped who I am, and I am eternally grateful.

Emily Sutherland ~ We had a bond from the moment we said hello. Your encouragement, coaching, and skill have taken this book from *pretty good* to what you hold in your hands. I am grateful that you have shared your talents with me.

I love each and every one of you more than I can put into words.

table of contents

introduction

This book is written for you. It doesn't matter what age you are, where you practice your faith, what street you grew up on, or how you identify in any way. In this book, you will find at least one thing on these pages that can change your life. You will find one piece of advice that I have been lucky enough to learn in my fifty-plus years that can help you to make your corner of the world a better place. And really, that's the best that most of us can do–make our corner of the world a better place.

Before we go any further, just know that the stories you will read on these pages are true, but in many cases, I have changed the names of the people in them. Thank you to all the dear people in my world that (sometimes unknowingly) comprise these stories that are so worth telling. Love you. Mean it.

Some of the lessons between these two covers come directly from journals, which I've kept my entire life. My high school journals were actually those small hardback diaries with the little lock on the side that, ironically, didn't lock. They were filled with thoughts and feelings about boys, friends, tears, and what I thought were big secrets and gigantic philosophies about life.

When I married Jeff and we started having babies, I journaled to our kids. Since Maia, Webster, and Georgia are now 20, 18, and 14, it's safe to say that I have written a lot of these lessons to them over the years. I've probably repeated myself a thousand times on those pages.

When I received my first breast cancer diagnosis in 2012, I did an online journal to communicate with those I love. Then Jeff was diagnosed with kidney cancer. During the years that followed the major cancer surgeries that saved our lives, life threw all kinds of things at us. Between the two of us, we had a hernia surgery, a reconstructed ankle, a colon resection, ovarian cysts that ruptured, vertigo fits, migraines, a hysterectomy, removal of non-cancerous tumors, a vasectomy, a lumbar puncture, and a bout of Transient Global Amnesia. Seriously, who gets amnesia?! People often call us *special.* Apparently being special is overrated. But we learned a lot and I journaled throughout the craziness.

Nearly six years ago, Jeff got diagnosed with Chronic Myeloid Leukemia. Shortly after that, I was diagnosed with a new primary breast cancer. Another online journal followed. I can't imagine how hard it has been for people to love us through all of this. But somehow they do. We are overwhelmed with the love and support of our community and family.

Within the pages of this book, I will share stories, excerpts from those journals, and a few of my own secrets. What I will not do is tell stories that aren't mine to share. So I will carefully walk that line to honor the people who have taught me so many important things.

Keep in mind that the things I learned from the stories you're about to read were impacted by where I was in life and the circumstances I was experiencing at the time. You may or may not resonate with everything or you may draw different conclusions based on where you are in life. We all experience life from unique vantage points, and we learn on a spectrum, not in silos. You may read the same things a year from now and see them completely differently. But, regardless, my goal is to share honestly about the people and experiences that have impacted my life in hopes that you will be inspired to look at your own relationships and circumstances for the wisdom and possibilities hiding below the surface.

Something you need to know about me is…I really like old people. You will read about some of my favorite lessons I have learned from people who have been around a lot longer than I have. Miss Bessie comes to mind. She was a Guest at Joy's House, the not-for-profit organization I was lucky enough to start nearly twenty-five years ago. (You also need to know that we always capitalize "Guest" to honor the people we serve. Guest is a proper noun around here.)

At 95 years of age, Bessie had the warmest and most contagious smile ever. And she used it often. Sometimes it was when her heart was bursting with love and it was the only way she knew to express herself since the stupid disease called Alzheimer's robbed her of the ability to use her words like she once did.

Sometimes she used her smile because she wanted something and she knew that if she changed the tone of her voice to be just a little bit softer, tilted her head slightly to one side, and pulled out that smile, she almost always got her way.

But sometimes around mid-afternoon, which is called *the sundowning period* in aging healthcare, she forgot to smile altogether. In fact, she said some pretty nasty things during these dark hours.

During one such sundowning period, Miss Bessie was in a mood. Everyone who crossed her path became a *witch*. In the interest of full disclosure, she used the *b-word*. I just didn't want to get this book banned from younger readers right off the bat. So we're going with *witch*, but you get the idea.

"What are you looking at, witch?" she spouted as someone walked by, barely glancing her way.

"Witch, I want to go outside!" she demanded to one of my coworkers like it was her first name.

It didn't matter who you were or what you were doing. In those moments, to Miss Bessie, you were a witch and she was going to let everyone know it. It was no secret that my coworker, Katie, had always been one of Miss Bessie's favorites, so when it was time to let Miss Bessie know that snacks were available, Katie was voted "Most Likely To Succeed" in getting her to join us.

Katie knelt down and, with softness and gentleness, said, "Miss Bessie, it's time to get a snack."

"So?" Miss Bessie shot back.

"Well, before we head in, I want you to tell me one nice thing," Katie smiled, deepening the rapport between the two and fueling the fire in their special way.

Miss Bessie stared her deep in the eyes and without missing a beat, she faintly smiled and said, "You look beautiful, you stupid witch. Now go get me a cookie."

Oh. My. Goodness. I. Love. Her. Miss Bessie taught me that filters are important, and I am going to cherish mine for as long as I have them. Because when they're gone, ugh… I am sure to scare away some people!

I love young people, too. So much. Reemphasizing the importance of filters was my son, Web. He was seven when I was diagnosed with my first breast cancer. My double mastectomy date was approaching quickly, and since my kids were nine, seven, and three years old, we had age-appropriate conversations with them about what was happening in my body and in our lives. While driving Web to school one day, with just the two of us in the car. I took the opportunity to ask him how he was feeling about the whole thing.

Web threw his hands into the air and began with, "Ehhhh…" He went on to tell me that he was worried that when the doctors took my bad cells, they would take my good cells, too.

I explained that they would do exactly that, but that they would keep enough of the good cells in my body so that I could live a healthy life. I also explained what a mastectomy is and that I would have new boobs, which I thought might startle him. But instead, he startled me.

He looked at me and sedately said, "That's okay. I don't really like the boobs you have now anyway."

Thanks. Thanks a lot. Again, cherish your filter while you have it, and use it wisely.

This is the kind of book where you can start on page 37, or you can read from beginning to end. You can write all over it or keep it in good condition so you can hand it off to someone else when you're done. You can use it as a guide when you want to facilitate a conversation with people in your life, or when you want a conversation starter with your sports team, youth ministry group, or club. Or you can keep every page as private as you would your own personal journal.

You should know before we get too far into this that I make no claims of being Mother of the Year. My kids are mostly grown at this point, and they are good people, but getting here wasn't always pretty and involved a lot of cursing.

I'm a pretty good wife. I could be nicer most days. And I interrogate myself often as a boss and as a friend. I'm a Christian, and I mess that up on a regular basis, too. So, just because I can share the wisdom found in this book doesn't mean I have mastered all the practices. Regardless, I am grateful for the lessons learned, from the youngest people in my life to those who claimed to be 93 but were actually 102. (You know who you are.)

I'm grateful you picked up this book and have read enough to get right here. Enough of this rambling, let's get on with it.

01

it's okay to be scared

Journal Entry — October 21, 2019

During the last week, my emotions have bounced all over the place. This past weekend, I was so tired that I just *couldn't*. I really just couldn't do anything. I was exhausted.

Now it's Tuesday and I'm angry. This afternoon's pre-surgery meetings with the physical therapist, breast surgeon, and oncology nurse were great. The information was helpful. Nothing went wrong. But when we got in the truck, my mood flipped. Jeff and I argued about something stupid. (Don't ask.)

I finally said, "I'm just really mad!" I went on to admit that I was angry we have to go through a major health crisis as a family again. I'm mad that our kids have had to face four (insert explicit) cancers with us.

I'm angry because when I asked the professionals today if this new breast cancer is the thing that will kill me, their eyes kind of moved around, looking for an answer, followed by, "Well..," "Um..." and, "We can't say for certain" or "It's hard to say."

I get it. They can't say anything with 100 percent certainty. I completely understand that. I also get that God is in charge. I get that a positive attitude goes a long way. I know prayers are powerful and that I have a lot to live for. I get it. I do.

But today, I'm angry. Really angry.

I'm also grateful. I'm especially grateful that, even when I was being nasty and biting earlier, Jeff grabbed my hand in the truck and said, "I'm scared too. But you and me...we've got this...together."

I half smiled, half cried, and said, "Somehow, I just have to stop thinking about what your second wife's name is going to be."

He sat silent for a moment like he was deep in thought, then he said, "Shakira."

Really?! Okay. I see how this is gonna go. With that, I reply:

Dearest Shakira,

I don't know who you are or where you are, but you need to step back. I may be a hot mess of emotions, but I'm not dead yet and I don't plan to be for a long time to come. It might be best if you go find your own man.

Warmly,
Jeff's first (and best) wife

02

you are as special as other people say you are

Years ago, my sister and I were having a conversation about some life changes she was going through, and I said, "You are as special as other people say you are."

My sister is special. She is beautiful and kind. She is smart and witty. She puts together these crazy outfits that somehow work perfectly on her. She has a smile that people long to see and gets great joy out of writing haikus. She is trustworthy and willing to do unusual things to make memories. She is downright wonderful.

I've known her since she was...well, born, but we weren't raised in the same house. We saw each other every other weekend, at most, because we share a dad and that was the visitation schedule. Now that I think about it, I don't really even remember when she was born. Man. That feels horrible to say. I was eight when she was born. She was born in July. My mom had my brother in October of that same year. And then my stepmom had my other brother the next July. Yep. I had three siblings born within twelve months. I'm positive this came up in therapy.

But really, I don't remember any of their births. I was alive. They weren't. Suddenly, they were. I grew up in the same house as my first brother, so we've always been close. But the other two took some time. Eight and nine years is a big difference between siblings who aren't raised in the same house. By the time they were playing on their new Game Boys, I wanted to see if I could get away with sneaking out of the house. By the time they were trying to sneak out of the house, I had been through grad school and had a big-girl job.

As they got older, the years between us seemed less important. My sister and I are the only two who live in the same city. She and I have shared a lot of time together as adults and we've grown closer than I ever knew I wanted. Now, I know I will cherish her for the rest of my life. I've gotten to know how wonderful she is and the things that make her so special.

During some of those life changes, however, she didn't see these things. She knew them, but it was like she had misplaced them and their memories were collecting dust. I heard her talk about not knowing if she was good enough to do the things she wanted to do next in her profession. She questioned relationships in her life. She just wasn't sure she was in the right place physically or emotionally.

She had forgotten about the time we were out and she stopped, mid-sentence, to help a stranger with his bags. He told her she was the only person who had offered to help and he'd been struggling for nearly an hour. She had forgotten how my kids would go from rolling around on the kitchen floor in I-hate-everything-in-this-world tantrums to screaming "TeTe!" with pure joy the moment she walked through the door, followed by an attack of hugs and giggles. (TeTe is the name my oldest gave her when was too little to pronounce "Aunt Corrina" and it stuck.)

When TeTe laughs, she *really* laughs. Her laugh begins almost like she's questioning whether or not she should be laughing in the first place. She usually looks around to see if others are laughing and when she sees that it's safe, she lets hers loose. If you happen to be sitting on a bench with her the moment her laugh breaks out, you'll be bouncing to the rhythm with her because the entire bench will shake. If you're wearing mascara, you might as well let it run because you won't be able to stop the tears streaming down your face.

When she was going through her moment of self-doubt, we sat down and made a list of her positive traits. After reading it together, that's when I breathed those words, "You are as special as other people say you are."

I'm pretty sure we all go through times of questioning ourselves. People can tell us about our special qualities our entire lives but, if you're anything like TeTe (or me) you probably brush them off with a smile and change the subject.

What would change if you realized that you are actually way more amazing than you ever realized? What would you do differently if you truly believed in the potential others see in you? Trust me, what you have to offer *is* so much better than you realize. I urge you to boldly pursue those ideas that light you up. Let yourself dream bigger about what's possible for you. I challenge you to live like it's all true. Because it is.

03

stop pretending

I've been on one cruise in my life. On that one cruise, I met a guy. His name was Francesco. He was adorable and fun. He was Italian. He was attentive and energetic. He was also a jerk. Like, the king of all jerks.

Before he was a jerk, he was wonderful. It so happened that Francesco and I lived 968 miles away from each other, but for those few days, we were captive on the same floating paradise. Our first few dates consisted of all things vacation. Beaches. Coconut drinks. Jet skis.

Snorkeling. Private islands and sunscreen. Movies have been made about weeks like this.

When the cruise came back to port, I remember that dramatic feeling of leaving something you have come to enjoy. We hugged for what seemed like days and we talked about visiting each other. I cried as I walked away and looked back to find him watching me. Either there was a cello playing in the distance or I've clearly watched too many movies because I heard sad music as he became a speck in the distance. It was *dramatic.*

We simply couldn't live without seeing each other again, so Francesco flew to Indianapolis to visit. My friends instantly fell in love with his exotic look and Italian charm. He won everyone over and I was no exception. With that, we planned my trip to Boston.

We met at a hotel outside of the city and I instantly knew something was different. I'm usually pretty good with intuition, but it was hard with Francesco. It's said that Italian men flirt naturally and make every woman they meet feel like she is the only woman in the room who matters. Yep. At least this is how he had made me feel before I saw him outside of that hotel.

At dinner that night, he told me that he was going to have to work while I was in town. Okay. I wasn't afraid to explore by myself. Then he said we had to stay at the hotel versus his place because his roommate was sick. Uh-huh. I certainly didn't want to get sick. He went on to tell me that we weren't staying near his work or his place because, well, blah blah blah blah blah blah…

Long story short, that man's roommate was his girlfriend! A woman he had been dating for years. Like since before the cruise. Jerk.

When this realization sunk in, I got up from the dinner table and walked outside. I was in a strange city where I knew no one except this man and, come to find out, I didn't really know him at all. This. This was actually the stuff that movies were made of. Sad movies. Scary movies. Movies that couldn't possibly have a good ending.

"Tell me why you were so wonderful on the cruise, and when you came to visit me, and now…now, this?" I begged with a mix of confusion and anger.

He looked at me with those gorgeous brown eyes that almost made me forget what was happening. Then his words helped snap me back into reality.

"I don't have to be wonderful. You're on my turf now." That was his response!

Wow. I was standing in front of this person, but I suddenly realized that I was by myself.

The next day, instead of sitting around feeling sad because I wasn't the good judge of character I thought I was, I went into the city on my own. Boston is beautiful. The rich history and architecture make you want to pause where you stand. I closed my eyes and thought about the countless people who had walked in the very spot where I stood. I suddenly didn't feel so alone anymore.

After getting to know the city for a few hours, my feet found their way to a park trail, which led to a bench. There was an older man sitting on the far end of the bench throwing stale hot dog buns to the birds. He nodded in my direction, indicating that I could join him. I sat down.

At first, there was some small talk about the weather and how we were both visiting the city. It didn't take long for my new friend on this park bench in the middle of Boston to tell me his name. Henry. That's such a great old-man name. Henry asked what brought me to Boston.

"A man," I admitted. "Actually, a boy pretending to be a man."

Henry laughed. He told me he used to be a boy pretending to be a man until he met his wife, whom he married nearly fifty years ago.

Henry was apparently a troublemaker when he was younger. He shared the story about a night when he and his buddies went out and stole street signs, then placed them in the yards of their high school teachers. He had stories about stealing alcohol from his parents and filling the bottles back up with water, and about the time that he snuck a girl into his bedroom, trying to be cool, then got scared when she pushed him back on the bed and tried to kiss him.

We laughed a lot, which was easy to do, and we ended up trading stories for over two hours. I shared stories of garage-hopping with friends on Friday nights to get us through the weekend. Oh, come on. Surely you know what garage-hopping is…when you drive around looking for an open garage, then turn off the car while someone jumps out and sneaks into the garage looking for alcohol. I'm not proud that I can explain this.

I also recalled the countless times my friends would hear a teacher utter words like, "Let's just say there's a train coming," and blurt out in unison, "There's a train coming!" Those poor teachers.

Henry and I talked about how we're all children pretending to be adults until we decide to stop pretending. Doing childish things happens. Making bad decisions happens. But the time to stop is when making a childish decision is clearly going to hurt someone else. Being a grownup requires stopping ourselves before making decisions that only benefit us.

After that trip, I never talked with Francesco again. I didn't want to talk with him, and he didn't want to talk with me. Simple as that and yet, there's more. Francesco was pretending to be something he wasn't. But what about me? I was pretending to not see the signs.

He never wanted copies of any pictures of us. (Yeah, I said copies. I'm old. Before social media, we made copies of pictures.) Why wouldn't this guy want copies of pictures? I looked really good in that bikini with that sarong around my waist and coconut drink in hand.

Also, he could only talk a couple of nights a week during a two-hour block of time. I'm going to guess that's when his "roommate" had yoga class.

Turns out, I didn't love Francesco in the least, but I *did* love Boston. I loved that time on that park bench with Henry and I was grateful for the reminder that even the most serious lapses in judgment can be redeemed if we learn something. I learned that it might seem easy to pretend, but ultimately the truth is our friend.

Francesco, if this book has somehow ended up in your hands and you're reading these words with a flush in your cheeks and faint memories of a girl and a cruise, it's okay. I wish you the best. I hope you learned from that situation and grew into a great man. And don't worry about me. I found my great man later. So we're good.

04

find the truth hidden in criticism

It sucks when someone says something harsh. Believe me, I know. If you are anything like me (and I sure hope you're not), you are tempted to respond to harsh criticism with anger or defiance. I'm a work in progress, my friend. Maybe you are, too. But you know who we could all learn a thing or two from? Asher.

Asher was in high school and had a nice group of close friends until the day one of the young women in the group decided she'd had enough of him. Her name was Sophie and she found Asher to be annoying. Yes, Asher talked a lot and his words came out fast. He didn't have much of a filter, so those fast words often burst out saying things most people try to bury deep inside. As the self-proclaimed leader of the friend group, she took action.

At first, she began to leave him out of invitations to do things. Every once in a while, Sophie would make hurtful comments. And Asher wasn't always innocent. Remember, he could be annoying. We've established that he said things that most of us wouldn't dare. The division between the two of them got bigger and her influence on the rest of the group got stronger.

One Thursday, Asher was sitting at a lunch table with John, one of the other guys from the group, when Sophie marched over. She looked directly at John, and said, "Are you going to sit here with him or are you going to choose the rest of the group?"

If I had been 17-year-old Asher, this situation would not have gone well. Shoot. Who am I kidding? If I had been 50-year-old Asher, I'm not sure it would have gone well. But Asher? He stopped what he was doing, turned to John, and said, "Go ahead. You shouldn't be punished for being my friend."

After a few days of heaviness passed, Asher asked Sophie if they could talk. He told her that he knows he can be obnoxious and annoying. He shared that his purpose in wanting to talk wasn't trying to get her to change her mind about him or influence the mindset of the group, but that he wanted to understand what he might be able to do differently so that he can learn from her and become the best version of himself.

From there, Asher forced himself to be quiet. She talked. He listened. They hung up.

Days went by and Asher sat alone at lunch instead of bellying up to the lunch table with his old friend group. Eventually, he started eating lunch in his truck to avoid the discomfort of it altogether.

He found himself deepening friendships with John (who did, by the way, leave that lunch table on that Thursday, but then started joining Asher for lunch in his truck) and some other guys who didn't mind his obnoxious and annoying moments. As time went on, those moments became fewer and far between.

While Sophie's communication method wasn't gentle, to say the least, Asher was wise enough at the ripe old age of 17 to understand something that has taken me much longer to comprehend. Hidden within her criticism of Asher was something true. He was able to look beyond how he *felt* when she said things and see that there was an opportunity to grow in ways no one else had been willing to tell him.

None of us can control how someone speaks to us, but we can be attuned enough to know when we are confronted with a truth that will make us better. And if more of us learn this and remain open to becoming better versions of ourselves, maybe the whole world gets a little bit better.

05

if you say things with confidence, people will believe you

Jeff and I love adventure. Years ago, we did this thing called Dinner in the Sky. It's exactly as it sounds. We joined 18 other people around a dinner table and a crane lifted us high into the air to enjoy our meal. Yep. You are reading this correctly.

Before strapping into the three-point harness, the first thing we did was go to the bathroom because, well, we were going to be strapped into a three-point harness and a giant crane was going to lift us high into the air to enjoy our meal.

Once we were settled (strapped) in, we got to know our fellow diners pretty quickly because, for just a moment, I believed this might be the way I would die. For some reason, it felt important to know the last people who would see me alive. Personally, the worst part for me was the crane lifting me into the air. My feet were dangling and felt like they might just disconnect from my legs. The wind was sweet at first, then it got a little chilly before it started whispering things like, "I've got you right where I want you. Go ahead. Try to escape."

When I realized the anxiety attack wasn't going to kill me either, I started breathing again and looked around. Our city from this vantage point was really beautiful. The buildings didn't look as big as they do from the ground. It was more like we were one of them rather than a speck on the sidewalk in their shadows. I could see things in the distance that I had only ever experienced at close range. It gave me chills to be sitting there looking out on places from this angle that I only knew from the streets.

In spite of the chatter from my tablemates and the sound of the chefs preparing our meal (we'll get to that in a moment), the stillness was surprisingly serene. So I settled in.

Chef handed me a pink drink with one of those cute little umbrellas in it. The sound of glasses clinking and our new friends saying *cheers* took over the stillness. We had reached our height and it was time to turn our attention to the chefs, as they introduced our meal for the evening.

"Welcome, everyone. For starters tonight we've prepared for you…"

Truth is…I wouldn't have a clue what this experience feels like because I've never actually done it. Don't you get mad at me! I'm trying to make a point here. While I'm certainly intrigued by the idea that people would thoroughly enjoy anything called Dinner in the Sky, my point in telling this story is…if you say things with enough confidence, people will believe you.

Be careful what you say. Be careful what you believe.

In spite of the fact that I've never done it, Dinner in the Sky is a real thing and a truly outstanding concept. Just search for them. And please, if you book an experience, let me know. I'd love to hear about it. I'll just do so with my feet planted firmly on the ground!

06

it's okay to laugh

The doctor called and said she wanted to see us. It was the year after my breast cancer diagnosis, so of course we went immediately. It didn't matter that her call came the day before Christmas Eve, or that my mom and stepdad were at our house to celebrate the holiday with our family of five. The doctor wanted to see us, so we went.

Jeff and I arrived early and were the only people in the waiting room as we waited as patiently as possible for the nurse to escort us back to meet with the doctor. I can still see the tenderness in the eyes of everyone who worked there. They knew what we were about to hear. Their gentle hellos and the way they turned away before we could engage in conversation should have been telling, but it wasn't. There is no way, just a year after my cancer diagnosis that we were getting bad news. No way.

A doctor's visit for us normally started with niceties because we adored our physician, and she adored us. But this time, *How are you? Big plans for the holiday?* and any other normal conversation topics were skipped. She didn't waste any time.

"Jeff, the spot you have on your kidney…I hate to tell you this, but I think it's cancer." She paused for a minute. There was a deafening silence. "I recommend seeing an oncologist as soon as possible." Her directness was important because if she had softened any of the words, I am confident we wouldn't have understood. Again, there was no way, just a year after my cancer diagnosis that we were getting bad news. But we were.

I looked at my husband with my eyes wide and made some kind of noise, maybe it was a sigh, out loud. I think I said his name softly as I reached out to put my hand on his. I can't remember exactly. He just stared ahead, looking at nothing.

I don't even remember walking out to our vehicle. I do remember the drive home. Jeff called his parents. His mom answered in her sweet voice and asked if everything was okay. Before Jeff could even say the first word, his voice cracked, and he handed me the phone. It was clear that he wasn't going to be able to say the words that needed to be spoken and so I said them for him.

"Our doctor strongly believes that Jeff has kidney cancer. We don't have next steps yet, but we're headed home now and will be at your place this evening." Having to share my cancer diagnosis with them had been terrible, but this was brutal. This was about their son, their firstborn child. I hope I never understand how horrible it was for them to hear those words.

I was driving. Jeff sat next to me. We didn't talk. We didn't have any more words.

The drive home brought us glimpses of twinkle lights strung up on people's homes. Christmas trees gently waved at us with sympathy as we drove by. The colors and decorations that usually bring peace and wonder during the holiday season became blurry as we got closer to home. Reality was sinking in. We were going to have to walk in the door and tell our kids that now both of their parents had been diagnosed with one of the scariest diseases of our lifetime.

We walked through the front door, greeted first by our dog, who wagged his tail with excitement like we had been gone for weeks. It was a familiar moment, and for a split second, everything felt like it was going to be okay.

But that feeling changed when our oldest, barely eleven, came around the corner. With a mixture of fear, strength, and panic, she asked, "Is it cancer?"

My mom stood behind her with her hands on Maia's shoulders. I think she was offering support or maybe just trying to get a closer look at our faces to understand what was happening. I shook my head yes and tried not to cry.

Within moments, we were all gathered into one room and trying to process the news. In those moments, it wasn't just about hearing that it was cancer as it was that we had just heard that word one year earlier. Jeff and I were each forty years old and thought we were in good health. This just didn't seem real. What were we supposed to do now?

First, we prayed together. Second, we cried together. Third, we packed our bags so we could drive to southern Indiana to be with Jeff's family and wake up with them on Christmas Eve.

Before heading out, we decided to open our presents to the kids and each other. I know, it sounds strange, but in those moments of fear and exhaustion, of confusion and love, sometimes you pick the easiest and most familiar road. On this day before Christmas Eve, that was the road we chose.

The Christmas tree lights were already on. The fire had been lit. The presents found their way underneath the tree. We were doing this, in spite of the cancer cloud that was looming about our heads. I remember thinking, *For just this small amount of time, Lord, let us enjoy these moments together. Let things feel normal for the next hour because I realize that we are far from normal once we step out of this house tonight.*

Also, let me be clear about something. I never wrap gifts early. I mean never, ever, ever. But on this particular Christmas, by some miracle, I had. I'm still shocked that I had finished the wrapping by the 23rd of December. We sat around the tree with the kids, handing out presents, and I couldn't remember anything that was under that tree.

One by one, the kids opened their gifts. Georgia, who was already funny at the age of four, squealed when she opened her first Furby toy. Maia forgot about every trouble in our world when she was gifted with the Lego Friends set. Web's highlight was a yo-yo that I don't think he ever really mastered, but I'm positive broke a lamp or two over time.

Drowning in red and green wrapping paper, we repeatedly paused for photos because capturing those moments felt important. It felt normal. I would say super mom-like things like "Wait a minute. Let me get the camera. Hold on! " as they continued to rip open gift after gift.

When Jeff picked up what was clearly some kind of a book to unwrap, I couldn't remember what it was. A cookbook? A survivalist guide? A book about Scotland? I couldn't, for the life of me, remember what it was.

Suffice it to say that I was just as surprised as he was when he removed the wrapping paper. The title was "1,000 Places to See Before You Die."

Oh. My. Goodness.

"Really, Tina? Really?!" was all he could say.

Tears shot from my eyes.

"I'm so…I don't…I didn't…" I stuttered. But I couldn't stop my stuttering from turning into laughter. Then the laughter morphed into some kind of strange tears and pretty soon, we were all laughing and crying.

That happened a solid decade ago and I still giggle every time I think about that moment. We cried a lot of scared tears that day, but the fact that we found humor in that moment is a memory I'll hold onto forever. As backup, just in case the memory fades, I was lucky enough to have that camera in hand and I snapped a picture.

In the forefront of this picture is my husband, book in hand, with his I've-clearly-been-crying-for-hours-face, asking in disbelief, "Really, Tina? Really?!" In the background of that picture is eleven-year-old Maia wearing an unfortunate red and cream striped shirt, hand on her forehead, with a combination of laughter and anguish on her face. Her smile is so big that her braces nearly outshine her youthful beauty. That photo reveals everything we were feeling at that moment.

No matter how bad things seem, it's okay to laugh. We make a lot of cancer jokes in our household. It makes other people uncomfortable and for that, I'm sorry. But for us, it's okay to laugh. We're still here. In part, we're probably still here because we *have* laughed along the way.

It's really a good thing Jeff is still alive because I'm pretty sure we haven't visited a single place that poorly timed gift said we *must* see before we die. If we ever do visit those places, I hope the memories we make are half as good as the one we made the day he opened that book.

07

other people have good ideas, too

Do you know who still gets this one wrong sometimes? Me. This girl. I'm not proud of that, but it's true.

My team at Joy's House recently completed the first part of a digital ecosystem project blah blah blah (I know I lost you at digital ecosystem) that we had been working on for over a year. It is big and innovative. As with most big and innovative projects, we were passionate about the things we were proposing to a group of stakeholders on a certain wintery Wednesday morning. And we were tired.

When we gathered with these stakeholders in person for the first time ever, comments like, "You're so much taller than you looked on Zoom!" and "I've really missed being in person!" were shared all around. There were only six of us, but we filled up the conference room table with computers, laughter, and possibilities.

After an hour of feedback on the project, Anthony leaned in and said, "I'd like to challenge that point."

A very short and powerful word shot out of my mouth.

"No." I cut him off and shut him down. "I don't put my foot down very often, but I'm putting it down right now."

What does that even mean? What was I putting my foot down about, you ask? It doesn't even matter. The fact is that I didn't give this poor man a chance to get out another thought. Was it because I was right? Or because I was *so important* that his perspective didn't matter? Nope. It's because I was being an idiot.

For a few hours after the meeting, I let myself marinate in my behavior. By the end of the day, I didn't like how I felt after shutting down his challenge…his perspective…his idea. So, I wrote an email to the group. It read:

Anthony,

I'd like to listen to what you were going to say at the meeting. Ugh. I don't want to, but I know I should. Can we blame my crass shutdown on exhaustion? (Insert goofy smiley face here.)

Let's make sure to talk about how this project might be made into the best version of what we need and want it to be.

Signed,
Sometimes I Can Be Idiotic

Do you know what we left with at the end of that meeting? The same exact thing we walked in with because I wasn't willing to listen to someone else's perspective. Nothing new or original, just my limited perspective. I might have still been right, but we'll never *really* know for sure. I didn't allow space for anyone else to bring something great to the conversation.

Why is it that we are so hesitant to stop and really listen to the ideas of others? I think it can be a lot of things. These might be a few:

- Our egos get in the way, and we want to believe that our ideas are best.
- Fresh ideas usually ride shotgun to change. And...
- Change makes us feel uneasy.
- New things force us to think about things differently.
- Some people try to sound smart by acting like they have all of the answers.
- Innovation often takes time, energy, and money.

That last one – innovation – sounds big, and what I'm talking about here can be huge. It can also be the smallest of things. Sure, you might actually invent highways for flying cars, or we might just be talking about the best way to get your dog to go potty somewhere other than in the corner of the living room.

Other people have good ideas, too. But if you act anything like I did that one day in that conference room, you'll simply never know.

Thank goodness the email I got back from Anthony said this:

> Hi Tina,
>
> It is no problem at all! I think it's important to take a stand on things that matter. Maybe this qualifies…who am I to judge?
>
> We can all be honest with one another. In my opinion, every preconceived

> notion should be analyzed to see if there
>
> are better conclusions to make.

Yep. He was right. I made a vow to do better in our next meeting and no one held my poor behavior against me.

I did, however, get another email as a follow-up to that meeting. It was from someone else who had been sitting around the table that day and it simply read:

> What has 5 toes and isn't your foot?
>
> My foot.

I'll be sure to come up with something better than putting my foot down the next time I decide to shut someone down. I simply can't handle the dad jokes.

08

advocate for yourself

Journal Entry — March 8, 2021

On November 22, 2020, I prepared for a surgery that I didn't recognize was going to be a beast. I got up that morning at 4:30 to shower with my pre-surgery antiseptic. If you know, you know. Just imagine scrubbing your body with something that smells like your neighbor burned a pile of leaves, turned the ashes into a pinkish-brownish antiseptic, and told you to slather it from head to toe in preparation for surgery.

I opened each of the kids' bedroom doors like when they were little and touched their feet, blew them a kiss, and shut the door behind me. Then we were off. Jeff drove and we checked in at 6:00 a.m. as instructed. We waited in a large room with white walls, cold chairs, a coffee machine that wasn't making coffee, and a bunch of other anxious-looking people.

A woman carrying an iPad looked down at what I assumed was a list and called my name. She asked Jeff and me to wait off to the side near a wall while she collected other patients. It felt like we were in school, lining up for gym class. The iPad lady then asked us to follow her.

Two by two we all walked down a hallway where hospital beds lined the walls with poorly typed notes that said something like, "Don't touch. These are saved for the unfortunate people walking down this hall to be butchered and then put back together. Seriously, don't touch. These are sanitary. Well, sort of. Because you just breathed all over them. Just keep walking." I may not have that exactly right, but it was something like that.

Curtains lined the area where we were directed, and we were each led into the space behind each curtain. That's when it was just Jeff and me again, behind our curtain. We sat with our anxiety until a slew of nurses, doctors, and other hospital personnel came in, asking questions and answering our questions.

Then *BOOM*... "My name is Chris. I'll be the nurse in surgery with you today. We're ready to go." *Okay, Chris. I guess we're doin' this thing.*

Jeff kissed me on the forehead and said a prayer with me, then Chris and I headed to travel down a long and quiet hall. Chris wheeled me into the operating room, which was sadly familiar. I had already had a number of surgeries during the previous months. But this operating room was pretty empty, unlike the one I was in during my first cancer surgery. That time, the medical team looked like the cast of *Grey's Anatomy,* and I remember thinking I'd like to have a drink with them if they weren't about to cut me open. But this room was pretty much the opposite.

I always ask for a moment to pray before they put me under anesthesia because: a) it seems like a good thing to do b) someone once told me that you actually recover faster if you are relaxed before going under. So, before the anesthesia kicked in, I prayed. Then they put the mask on my face. I lied there. I waited. I prayed again. Then I thought, *Wait. This isn't working. Something's wrong.* I said some of those words out loud and saw Chris open his mouth to respond. That's the last thing I remember.

My next memory was trying to come out of the anesthesia. I was in recovery for a couple of hours, but I didn't know that. My memories of that time were short and scattered and went something like this:

"Your surgery was nearly eleven hours long." *Something must have gone wrong. It shouldn't have taken that long.* Eyes shut.

"Tina. Tina. Can you hear me?" *No. I can't. Have to sleep.*

"We have a GSW [gunshot wound] coming in." *I don't know if that's real. I hope it's not real.*

I heard myself say, "I'm scared. Am I okay? I'm really scared."

I felt Jeff grab my hand. I went back to sleep. Everything was going to be okay.

"I'm so sorry, but your husband had to leave. We have limited visitation hours because of the pandemic." *Are those tears?*

I was really scared. I didn't know if I was okay. I had questions about why the surgery had taken so long. I remember reaching for Jeff's hand before he left saying, "I don't want you to go." But he *had* to leave. I lay in that recovery bed and worried about the gunshot wound victim if, in fact, there actually was one.

After a number of days in the hospital, I went home and entered a long recovery period. My surgery had been a *DIEP flap* which means, in short, I had a fresh cut from hip to hip and both of my breasts looked way more *interesting* than they had ever been before. Also, to be clear, I've had something like four or five sets of boobs at this point, so there's been a lot to compare to over the years.

Today is March 8. Scars are formed where the cuts were. I've had yet another surgery for reconstruction since that November marathon surgery. Reconstruction was only two hours long and I was back at home by dinner. Cool. Fine.

But last night something didn't seem right. I ended up in the emergency room at my local hospital. They agreed that it was critical to get in to see my surgeon the next morning to discuss a possible infection in my reconstruction surgery site. That means today–*this* morning.

I called as soon as the office was open. Granted, it was first thing on a Monday, and I know they're slammed, so I left voicemails in a couple of places. After dropping my son off at school, I headed toward my surgeon's office. Knowing that it is rude to show up unannounced, I called and waited until I got a human on the phone. There were a lot of nice exchanges during our conversation, but this is pretty much how it went:

Vicky: "Alright, Mrs. McIntosh, we can get you in with Terry tomorrow at 3:00."

Me: "I understand, but I really need to be seen today."

Vicky: "Yes. Unfortunately, there is nothing open on the schedule until tomorrow."

Me: "Cool. I get it. But you should know that I'm headed that way now and need to be seen today."

Vicky: "I simply don't have the authority to make that happen."

Me: "Yep. I'm still headed that way and have faith that I'll be seen today. I appreciate your help."

As I was walking into the office, I took some deep breaths and prayed that God would guide my steps and my mouth, because fear and anxiety can make me say some pretty stupid things. This is how that exchange went with Lady-At-The-Window (whom I will call LATW):

LATW: "Hi. Can I help you?"

Me: "You know that lady who marches in and demands to be seen? Well, I'm the nice version of that lady. Please have some mercy and grace on me. I need to be seen today."

After explaining everything, LATW couldn't have been any nicer or more helpful. By the grace of God, my nurse had come in early and got me back almost immediately.

She confirmed that I have an infection in my left breast, she ordered antibiotics for me to start immediately. Then she told me not to wait so long to come in if I think I might have an infection in the future. If she only knew.

09

keep hand warmers in your car

It was so late on a Saturday night that it was actually really early on a Sunday morning when I was driving through Indianapolis. Regardless, the reason I was out late was that I worked as an event planner, and I loved it. My biggest client was the Indianapolis Colts and whenever we had a home game, I spent my weekend setting up and tearing down events, which usually involved late nights and early mornings. I was a little fish in that big pond, and it sure was fun to swim there.

There were some constants outside of the stadium where these Colts events took place. Some I loved and some, not so much. There was Tiny, who was, ironically, not at all tiny. Tiny was a 35' tall blow-up character who wore a Colts jersey (duh) and held up the pointer finger of his right hand because the Colts were definitely #1. Blowing him up felt like I imagine it might feel trying to hold up the earth. The slightest wind would cause Tiny to slump over to one side and whoever was unfortunate enough to be standing on that side of him would inevitably panic, convinced that Tiny was going to swallow them whole. I was sure he was coming for me sooner or later, and that would be my demise.

Another Colts' stadium constant was Fly Guys. These are the same stupid things you see flying on every used car lot in America. I. Can't. Stand. Fly Guys. They're sloppy. They're dirty. They try to intimidate passersby. As a matter of fact, I dislike them so much that I occasionally get sidetracked yammering on and on about my dislike for them. My disdain for them was no secret.

One Monday morning, I came into the office in a happy-go-lucky mood until the moment I discovered a horrid six-inch tall, battery-operated, red-like-the-devil Fly Guy sitting on my desk. It was on. We locked eyes. He did his annoying dance, obviously looking for a fight. And I was ready for one. Clearly, my coworker thought this little joke would be hilarious.

Without skipping a beat, I stepped into my office like nothing was happening. I casually reached into my top right drawer, felt the smooth edge of the scissors with my fingers, and exercised my revenge.

Sparing you the gory details, I'll just say this: Fly Guy never danced again. He did, however, find his way to my coworker's office–an arm here, a leg there, an unidentifiable piece of red somewhere else. That's right, Fly Guy, don't you dare mess with me again.

Since I can't sit in negativity for too long (or it consumes me), let's go back to the more positive aspects of those days. It was such a fun time to be involved with the Colts' organization. Energy was high. We were winning games. Peyton Manning was our quarterback, and his teammates were incredible players and stellar people. Colts blue flooded the city of Indianapolis with a hum of energy that spilled into every corner of the state of Indiana.

I was 27 and single then. I developed friendships with people I met along the way, one of whom will be like a sister until the day we die. Together, we would set up for events, enjoy the bands, meet people, laugh, make new memories, laugh a bit more. Tear down. Repeat at the next event. And we froze a little most weeks. (It gets cold in Indiana during football season.)

I'm sure this is where you might expect me to talk about the life lesson: always keep hand warmers in the car. And, you know, it's good advice. But that's not the most important reason for this tip.

Being on the streets of Indianapolis at 3:00 in the morning opened my eyes to things I might have normally breezed by during the busy days–things I might have missed while wrangling Tiny and pondering the evils of Fly Guys. After setting up in the same spot week after week, I realized that some of the people in this area were not coming and going. They weren't all here to visit the stadium. Some were here because they *lived* here.

I was struck by the number of people sleeping on the streets, especially in the cold weather. In my city. Right on the same streets where thousands of fans, media crews, NFL VIPs, and people like me swarmed around them fresh from our comfortable homes in cozy, warm clothes. It's heartbreaking.

I observed the responses of people walking by someone living on the streets. Many avoided making eye contact with someone sitting with a cup in hand. That didn't feel possible for me. I *had* to make eye contact. Give a head nod. Say hello.

Marcus was one of those guys. He was an older man. Short hair, usually covered by a stocking cap. A warm smile and beautiful eyes.

One middle-of-the-night-early morning, when our event setup was done, I had a few moments to sit and catch my breath. I spotted Marcus sitting on a concrete ledge nearby.

"Can I join you?" I asked.

He nodded and a conversation ensued that would take about 20 minutes but would last a lifetime. Marcus openly admitted that he was an alcoholic. His drinking had led him to life on the streets. He had lost his wife and children. He thought he might have grandchildren, but he wasn't quite sure–he thought he saw them once walking into a restaurant.

Marcus had a few worldly possessions and a tent set up not far from where we were sitting, which he slept in most of the time. He was surrounded by a small community of others, and they looked out for each other. He had blankets, but not enough for the cold Indiana winter. His hands were always cold. He had some clothes, but never enough socks, some dishware, and a few other necessities.

He explained that his drinking had led him to this place, yet he wasn't going to stop drinking. This life wasn't ideal, but he was oddly at peace with it. I asked him what he would do with the money people dropped into his cup that day. He broke eye contact and looked down and the ground for a minute.

Then, after straightening himself up a bit, he said, "Probably buy a fifth." I appreciated his honesty.

Then he asked about my life and I shared a few things about myself before I had to get back to work. I loved those 20 minutes together and now, because of Marcus, I always have a bag tucked under the driver's seat of my car packed with all kinds of things he told me were important, including soap, washcloths, and lip balm.

And hand warmers. Always hand warmers. I call it my Marcus Bag.

Marcus may or may not remember me after all these years, but I remember him. I realize that I can't *save* every person. I'm at peace with that. What I can do, however, is *see them.* I can make eye contact. I can nod. I can say hello. These people we see in tents, or sitting on the sidewalk, or pushing a cart, or standing at the intersections…they're humans. For that reason alone, they deserve to be *seen.*

When my kids were younger, whenever we'd roll up to an intersection where someone was panhandling, they would cringe as I started putting down my window. They knew what was coming. But they stopped rolling their eyes at me the day we came to an intersection and got close enough to read the scribbled print on a torn piece of cardboard a man was holding. *Out of work. In need of soap, washcloths, and lip balm.*

I reached into my Marcus Bag and pulled out everything on this man's list. The light was getting ready to turn green when I said, "I have one more thing!" and I eagerly pulled out hand warmers to place in the palm of his chilly hands.

10

don’t expect everything you need from one person

Bridal showers all share one primary agenda. To shower the bride with things she’ll need for her new life. I’ve been to dozens of showers and there are seemingly endless ways this agenda is accomplished that are intended to add an extra element of fun to the occasion. Sometimes there’s a theme, like everyone wears a shade of pink. (Those are maybe my least favorite.) Often there are games where you have to do silly things or answer awkward questions. I’ve answered everything from, “What’s the bride’s most hated chore?” to “How old was she when she had her first proper kiss?" (Some of them got a little more risqué, but I'll spare you those memories.)

What I like most about bridal showers are the relationships. It's beautiful to see a group of women come together to celebrate another woman. The hugs are covered in *I'm so happy for you* whispers. Families begin to merge in unexpected ways. Old friendships are celebrated. New friendships begin to form, and you know it because of the bright tone in their voices when they say, "See you at the wedding!" as they head out the door with a smile.

At my own bridal shower, more than 20 years ago now, we did a lot of the traditional shower activities. I remember eating great food, being wrapped in toilet paper for some reason, and being cautious when opening presents because folklore insists that every broken ribbon signifies a child in the bride's future. One broken ribbon means one child. Twelve broken ribbons? Twelve kids. I liked kids, but twelve of them? Help.

Before leaving my bridal shower, everyone was asked to write down a piece of advice for me to read later. Some of them made me laugh. *Beauty and his eyesight will fade. Only fight naked.* Some were heavier. *Always remember that you're on the same team. Never go to bed mad.*

There was, however, one piece of advice that has impacted my marriage more than any other. The handwriting was a combination of print and cursive, written so small that I had to squint to read it. The handwriting alone told me that someone aged had written it. I imagined her hand holding the pen. Wrinkles on a soft hand that looked like ocean waves on a sunny day and that same sun having colored her skin with shades of ivory and brown. Nails cut short with a shade of red nail polish probably named something like *Cherry Blossom* writing these words with such ease, likely never knowing how much they would change my life…

Don't expect everything you need from one person.

I didn't fully get it at the time. I was preparing to marry the best person I had ever met. Certainly, he was going to provide everything I would ever need until the end of time.

I'd always dreamed of growing up and marrying someone who would be my best friend, my partner in life, the father of my children, my roommate, my financial teammate, my emotional support, and my…everything.

But after the wedding? I got it. This woman's advice was genius.

My husband can fix just about anything. He's also the guy you want on your team when playing a trivia game. He is the first person to show up when you have a flat tire. He is a natural-born teacher, loves God, and has strength beyond his years. But if you need to hear the words, "That must have been really hard for you," or "That would make me sad too," he's not your guy. As incredible as he is, when I need empathy, I call a friend.

I know who will let me sit with my sorrow. I know who will ask questions that help me help myself through the moment. I know who will stand a little taller and who will have my back should a fight break out. I've got friends for every occasion - both the hard occasions and celebrations. These are my best friends, my chosen sisters. They do not take anything away from the importance of Jeff's essential presence in my life. But having them to lean on does take a lot of pressure off of him.

The rest of the advice I received at my bridal shower is all true. We are on the same team. His eyesight and my external beauty have faded. We've learned to not go to bed mad. And we only fight naked. Or we did until our neighbors filed complaints.

But seriously, this wise woman's advice has proven to be a game-changer. Expecting my husband to be a superhero, even if he is the best human being I know, isn't fair to him. And, as independent and strong as I know I am, I require a lot of support to survive and thrive. If I expected my husband (God bless him) to meet my every need, we wouldn't have made it a week.

11

learn how to be a good friend

I'm not convinced that being a good friend comes naturally to most of us. I'd like to think it does, but I'm just not sure. When I was little, everyone was my friend. As long as the boy next to me would share his toys, he was in.

I noticed the same trend when my kids were young. I used to love when my kids would tell me something about their "new best friend." If I followed up by asking, "What's your friend's name?" the answer was almost always, "I dunno." It just didn't matter. The other little dude shared his Legos, so they were friends. Simple as that.

As I got a little older, friendship became more about shared interests and trust. Close relationships formed and if a friend had my back for just about anything, then we were tight. Oh, and gender started to come into play. Boys usually hung out with the other boys and girls often found our circle of girlfriends.

It's during the teen years when things get deeper for most of us. These important years hopefully taught us some things about how to be a good friend. If you're anything like me, you probably made a few mistakes and also some lifelong friends along the way.

In high school, I had my closest group of friends and yet, I was friends with a lot of other people. As much as I'd like to think I was a good friend to so many others, those little fake-lock diaries, which I now keep in a plastic bin in a spare closet, tell a different story about the teenager I was in weaker moments.

I talked about people behind their backs more than I wish I had. I was jealous of so many people for so many reasons. I rarely had the emotional intelligence to consider that other people had things going on in their lives that would impact how they acted on any given day. I should have had mercy on them. I should have shown them kindness. Heaven forbid another girl would look at the guy I was talking with. Darts, man. I could shoot darts out of my eyes. And my words had the potential to be sharp.

Let's not forget that my formative years happened during the mid to late 80s. I actually think I learned how to be a friend from John Hughes' movies. Now that I think about it, it could be worse. John Hughes' movies showed me what could happen if I kept backstabbing other people.

I had my own stuff going on, too. I victimized myself after my parents' divorces and for other things I'm not going to put in print, but I had my own issues and sometimes I allowed them to swallow my kindness and spit out ugly things. I'm not proud of my choices in those moments, but I can't go back. So I've tried to learn from them.

Not long ago, after I posted some high school pictures on Facebook, I got a message from a friend from high school. She and I ran in the same circles back then. Or rather, our circles overlapped. We weren't incredibly tight and we don't really keep in touch, although she crosses my mind on occasion. We messaged about how quickly life goes by and how we find it hard to believe that we are in our fifties. We talked about our lives now, our families, and the things we do in our spare time. Then she wrote something that made me pause.

> Life goes so fast…seeing those pictures was nostalgic. It was also hard. High school was really hard for me. It may have seemed like I was snooty or that I had it all together, but I didn't. I never felt like I belonged. I felt like everyone hated me. And inside, I was broken. I know it was so long ago, but it still hurts.

My first response was to tell her that she was wrong about how she behaved or came across to others. But, after thinking about it, who was I to tell her how she should feel or how others perceived her? Instead, this was my response:

> I understand what you're saying. I will
>
> also tell you this - we were all broken
>
> and misunderstood in our own ways.
>
> And if there is someone who doesn't
>
> understand that as teenagers, we
>
> couldn't...just couldn't...then they don't
>
> deserve the space in our lives. I'm sorry
>
> that your perception of yourself in high
>
> school was anything less than the
>
> beautiful and kind person that you are.
>
> I've always had a place for you in my
>
> heart. I'm so glad you texted me and

shared all of this. Here is my unsolicited
advice - forgive that teen girl for the
ways she acted and felt. She had it hard
and she didn't know who she was yet.
But *this you*...wow. *This you* is wonderful
and I can only imagine how fulfilled you
are now and how you show up in all of
the right places.

As I stared at my phone, I saw the three dots. They were moving. She was getting ready to write something. I waited, hoping that I hadn't crossed a line. The time was 10:10 a.m.

One minute passed. Two minutes. Then five. The dots went away and I sat there wondering how I could recover from saying something when maybe I should have just sent a virtual hug.

At 10:38 a.m., I got a notification. She had written back. It read:

> Thank you so much. I just had to step away and ugly cry for a minute. Thank you for your kindness.🩶

Wouldn't it be great if there was a checklist to follow that helps us know how to be a good friend? What if we could refer to this list when we need to make sure that we are living up to the expectations that come with friendship? I don't know about you, but I could use a refresher course every few years because that teenage girl is still alive and well in this fifty-some-year-old body. That checklist might look something like this:

- √ Be trustworthy. Don't share your friend's secrets with anyone else – *ever.*
- √ Don't talk negatively about your friend.
- √ Listen to your friend and offer feedback only when appropriate or asked.

√ Apologize when you make a mistake and accept an apology when one is made to you.

√ Be honest without being mean or spiteful.

√ Be open and accepting of your friend's changes and growth.

√ Be fun and share new adventures.

On that day, when my high school friend reached out, I wish I could have reached through that phone at 10:38 a.m. to give her the biggest of hugs. I couldn't, so I sat there imagining the decades of pain she had just released from her spirit.

Then I sat back and had my own ugly cry. I thought about who I was in my not-so-great moments and I decided to forgive my teenage self for all of the times she didn't get it right and when she just didn't know how to show up.

Learning how to be a good friend is a gift to others. And a gift to ourselves. It's worth a bit of reflection and might require having mercy on ourselves and others. Because friendship is one of those rare treasures that nothing else in life can replace.

12

put down your phone

One day while I was working, I got a call from a friend who was on the verge of tears. Her babysitter had a fever and couldn't watch her seven-month-old.

"I don't know what to do. I understand that your schedule is crazy, but is there any chance you can come over and watch Jackson for two hours? I just can't miss this appointment again," she begged.

"Of course," I said. "I'll be right there."

I grabbed my phone and a list of people I needed to get a hold of that afternoon, then I was on my way. Once I arrived at the house, she gave me the rundown on Jackson and told me he almost always went down for an hour-long nap around 1:00 p.m. Got it. That meant that I had about thirty minutes until I could start checking off my to-do list.

It was a great thirty minutes. Jackson showed me all of his new tricks. He had started rolling over since I last saw him and could nearly sit up on his own. Whatever I had in my hands, he wanted. He was adorable. The time with him was refreshing for me.

Like clockwork, he started to rub his eyes and get a little cranky at about 12:50, so I changed his diaper, closed the blinds in his room, and tucked him into this crib. Back in the living room, I set up a makeshift office with my list of names and started going to work. Jackson was crying a little, but I reminded myself that babies soothe themselves and that he would go to sleep soon.

1:08 Still crying. I went in to check on him. He was sad but fine.

1:17 Still crying. I stood outside his door, wanting to make sure he was really okay. I mean, he wasn't my kid. I was worried that something was wrong and that it was my fault.

1:20 Still crying.

I weakened and went in. As soon as he saw me, he smiled. I'm such a sucker. I picked up that sweet boy and took him back to the couch. I swaddled him in the soft green blanket with his name stitched across the middle and snuggled him into my arms. The way he looked at me made me forget my schedule and oh-so-important work and guided me down memory lane about my own kids' nap times.

I remembered singing songs to them before they went to sleep, rocking them in our cream-colored glider with a little footstool, tucking them into their cribs then placing my hand on their chest to help them feel secure as they were drifting off to sleep, then slowly removed my hand as I backed gently out of the room. I remembered watching them as they slept and thinking how amazing the gift of life is.

That moment with Jackson was no different. Watching his eyes get heavy made me yawn and I felt my body relax with his. He had fallen fast asleep and nothing else in the world mattered at that moment. I stared at his chubby little cheeks and his perfect lips, parted just enough so that I could hear his breathing. I couldn't remember the last time I had relaxed like this.

I was lost in my thoughts about how quickly time really does go by and the stages of my own children's lives when I heard the garage door open. Jackson's mom came into the living room and smiled.

"Sucker?" She whispered with a smile.

"Yep." He was too cute. What can I say? I handed her perfect child to her and gathered my things to leave.

As I was walking out the door, my friend said, "I hope you were able to get some work done."

I just smiled. I didn't have the heart to tell her that I got absolutely no work done. She would have worried and felt bad for asking me to come over. But really, the time I spent with Jackson was far more valuable than anything else I could have spent time doing on my phone.

I get it. We have more technology on our cell phones than all of NASA's combined computing in 1969. For those who don't recall the significance of this date, that is the year that man first set foot on the moon.

I was born three years later. To those of you who were also alive during that time period, let's not start the debate on whether or not we really sent a man to the moon. That's a whole different book; one that I will not be writing.

Point is, we can do everything on our phones – run businesses, get degrees, entertain, create, write, publish, host events, and keep in touch with people all over the world. Everything…*except* connect with the people who are right in front of us.

Put it down. Look someone in the eyes, rock a baby, snuggle a pet, or do pretty much anything that can't be done on a phone. You will not regret it.

13

learn from others

The work we do at Joy's House is serious. Our mission is twofold: Adult Day Services and Caregiver Support and Education. On the adult day side, we are a community and safe place for people living with life-altering diagnoses. Our Guests are living with everything from Alzheimer's and other dementias to multiple sclerosis, strokes, traumatic brain injuries, Down syndrome, and other conditions requiring extra support. They come to visit Monday through Friday between normal business hours. The number of days they come each week depends on what they need and want.

Our days are filled with heavy and serious things, such as assisting Guests with toileting, giving cues to encourage them to exercise and join in with group events, assisting them with walking and transferring (moving from one location to another), medication reminders, and general safety. Our days are also filled with some of the best moments. Allow me to introduce you to three people—Mr. Willie, Mr. Dan, and Miss Irene—whose names first pop into my mind when I think about some of the good times at Joy's House over the last nearly twenty-five years and what I've learned as a result.

Mr. Willie loves jazz and has been a tap dancer all his life. So we threw Mr. Willie a jazzy tap party. We turned Joy's House into a jazz club with a stage at the front of one of our larger rooms and black draping around the room. Candles were "lit" (battery operated for safety, of course) and Guests were greeted by name as they entered our jazz club, where a legendary local jazz duo would entertain us. We wanted to include people and things that he loved since this day was designed to celebrate him, so Mr. Willie's family joined us.

Mr. Willie was presented with new tap shoes. It's an interesting thing about dementia…a lot of those long-term memories stay with us. He remembered tap shoes. The minute he slipped those shoes on, it was like a switch flipped inside of him. He danced for hours on that stage, playing to the audience, and sharing with us not only his talent, but a glimpse of what life was like for him before we came to know him at Joy's House. His family couldn't stop smiling as they danced and laughed alongside him. It was glorious.

Mr. Willie taught me to cherish the things that bring me joy in life.

Mr. Dan was hilarious. He had been diagnosed with Parkinson's disease in his forties. As time went on, he needed help with a lot of things, such as eating, using the restroom, and picking things up when dropped on the floor (many of which I think he did on purpose so we would pick them up for him). What he *didn't* need help with was being ornery.

I could be touring the biggest potential donor through Joy's House, and Mr. Dan would flat-out lie and tell the donor we had a kegger party the night before. One day, he and a couple of other Guests ("the guys") called me to the main floor. I went running because I thought something terrible was happening. They proceeded to shoot me with ping pong ball guns and laughed until I'm pretty sure they all peed themselves. Serves them right. They were rotten! Completely rotten and some of the best humans I've been blessed to know.

One year, in preparation for his wedding anniversary, Mr. Dan asked my coworker and me to help him pull off a surprise dinner for his wife. He needed us to be his arms and legs. He was bossy. The table had to be set with linens and two dozen red roses. Dinner was to include parmesan-crusted tilapia, asparagus, and just the right wine. All of the finest details, right down to the diamond necklace he had purchased for her. His neighbor even played the guitar and serenaded them during the meal.

As time went on, Mr. Dan's body began failing him more and more. At the end of his life, what would take you and me ten seconds to discuss took Mr. Dan and me ten minutes. He wasn't always happy-go-lucky, but he sure taught me a lot about being alive during a rough diagnosis. He taught me how to belly laugh, put together a puzzle, feed the birds, and be ornery. But the biggest lesson he taught me was how to keep your independence even when you have to depend on other people.

Miss Irene was living with Alzheimer's disease. When I first met her, she knew about her diagnosis, and we would sit for hours and talk about how she was feeling. She shared her fears, love for her family, and memories that she didn't want to lose.

On a good day, she loved to help others at Joy's House. She would help set the table for lunch and was a cheerleader for everyone around her. On a rough day, however, she did more sitting and stayed quieter than normal. I will forever remember one of those rough days. She was recalling to me the experience of receiving her diagnosis.

She told me, "I thought I'd die. I cried and cried. Everybody cried. And um…and…um…it's kind of hard on this one... I, um, didn't know what to do. I just thought I was going to die…but I didn't. And I'm still here." Neither one of us got through that conversation without breaking into tears. We just sat there together, holding hands, crying. She was lovely. Just lovely.

Years later, when Miss Irene passed away, I was sitting in the back of the room during her memorial service and the minister was sharing stories of her life. Then he stopped and said, "Thank God, Irene is now free. She is free from Alzheimer's disease, which took her from us so many years ago. After all, the person that Irene has been for the last seven years is not the person that we have all known and loved."

I almost stood up and shouted, "*That Irene*–the one with Alzheimer's. That is the *only* Irene I ever knew, and I loved her!" I have no doubt that the person she was before I met her was insanely wonderful because even *with* this nasty thief of a disease, she was still incredible.

Irene taught me that you are always valuable and worthy of love, even when you aren't yourself.

The Guests and the thousands of others who come to Joy's House for services may only be with us for months or years if we're lucky, but they will be a part of the Joy's House family for eternity. They are part of who we are as an organization, they are a part of the DNA at Joy's House, and they are a part of who I have become. I hope the person I continue to be in this life would make them proud. I hope they could look at me and say, "I taught her that."

We live in a world where it's easy for some people to get overlooked or drowned out by all the things that distract us. But if we pay attention, we can learn something from everyone we encounter. And those lessons can be especially joyful and life-changing because learning from people is not only good for us...it's good for them, too.

14

everyone has survived something

When I was diagnosed with my first cancer, Jeff and I decided to have age-appropriate conversations with our kids because we recognized that what we would tell our nine-year-old and our seven-year-old, needed to be different than what we would tell our three-year-old. So, we planned to tell our sweet little three-year-old, Georgia, what was happening when physical changes started taking place. In other words, we were going to wait until I had surgery. It was only thirty days away and a lot can happen in thirty days.

It was somewhat of a relief because she was arguably the only person in my life who loved me and who didn't know that I had received the diagnosis. I felt a sort of freedom when I was with her.

However, one day after getting out of my yes-I'm-a-40-year-old-mother-of-three minivan, Georgia looked at me and said, "Mommy, what's in your body?" She knew. At the age of three, she had heard or witnessed, or somehow just *knew* that something was wrong.

"Oh, Honey," I said, "It's called cancer." She looked at me with those captivating brown eyes and I could tell she had a lot of questions. I continued, "Our bodies are made up of good cells and unfortunately, Mommy has some bad cells." She looked at my breast where I had worn a Band-Aid after my biopsy less than thirty days ago. A lot can happen in thirty days.

She patted her own chest and said, "I only have good cells?"

'That's right, Georgia. You only have good cells. And you didn't give this to me and you can't get it from me. But guess what. The doctors are going to take out Mommy's bad cells."

Her eyes got big and she squealed with excitement. "Are you gonna cry, Ma Ma?

"I'm not going to cry right now," I told her.

"Oh", she said, "You're gonna cry at the doctor?"

"Probably, Georgia."

A few weeks of more questions from all of the kids went by and I decided that I was going to schedule date days with each of them before my double mastectomy. My date day with Georgia happened to be a beautiful Indiana day in May. The clouds had cleared, the sky was blue, and spring was happening. It was the kind of day when the birds are singing and flowers are popping up in all of the places.

Before we headed for the zoo, we had to make a stop at the hospital for some pre-surgery stuff. I talked with my nurse, signed papers, and had what felt like enough blood drawn to test for every condition known to modern medicine. Georgia and I turned in our valet ticket to the medical center's free patient valet and sat on a bench outside waiting for my cool minivan to come around the corner.

I wasn't in a feel-sorry-for-myself kind of mood. On the contrary, I felt proud. I had on my new *Fight Like a Girl* tank top, and an unsweetened iced tea in hand. I had just shown Georgia where they were going to fix Mommy, and I was ready to take on the next big adventure with my little girl. The zoo was waiting. The weather was perfect. We were ready.

Georgia had other plans, at least for a few minutes. An older gentleman sitting next to us was doing a crossword puzzle. Georgia turned to the crossword puzzle man and said, "What's your name?"

"Bill," he said.

"I'm Georgia!" She said in a voice so loud that everyone within a city block knew who she was.

Immediately, Bill turned to me. "I'm Georgia's mom, Tina. Hi."

Bill had a charisma about him that drew me in immediately. Soon, I knew some things about him. He was from northern Indiana. He lived an hour and a half away from this hospital and made the drive back and forth between his home and the hospital several days a week. I knew he had a son who got divorced a few years back and that the same son had two children. I knew he liked horses and hated creamer in his coffee.

I also learned that last month, his wife had made that hour-and-a-half drive with him, but she would never do that again. Again, I say to you, a lot can change in thirty days.

Bill shared that he had been coming to IU Simon Cancer Center for chemo treatments for nearly a year now. Last month, he was snuggled into the passenger's seat, half awake, half asleep, listening to his wife sing along to the 60s music on the radio. He loved it when she was driving because she focused on the road and got lost in her thoughts, which meant that she didn't usually realize when she was singing. He *loved* to hear her sing. She didn't sing often enough from his perspective.

He was drifting off in a post-chemo sleep when she half whispered, half screamed, "Something doesn't feel right." She pulled off to the side of the road and they switched places. Bill's adrenaline kicked in and he drove straight to the nearest hospital.

Racing to the emergency entrance, panic set in. She was having a heart attack. He knew it. She had been having heartburn, but she brushed it off thinking the cause was all the different foods given to them by their thoughtful friends during this stupid cancer battle. She had been tired, but who wouldn't be? She had been running him around since his first chemo treatment.

Bill's beloved wife was swept up by thoughtful and caring people the moment they pulled to the entrance. They asked a lot of questions and Bill pushed through his exhaustion to share all of the answers.

Bill was beyond eager to just be with his bride. A nice young woman wearing scrubs led him back to her room and he turned the corner to see her resting, hooked up to too many machines with wires dripping off of her arms and chest. Bill pulled up a chair and sat down next to the bed. He scooted himself even closer and reached for her hand. Just an hour before, *he* had been lying in a hospital bed, hooked up to too many machines with wires dripping off of his arms and chest. And s*he* had reached for *his* hand to comfort him then.

He squeezed her hand. He thought he felt her squeeze it back. Bill looked at her face and wished he could hear her sing, or just hear her voice. He kissed the back of her hand and held it to his face, holding it there for what would have been a moment too long if she had been awake.

Later that day, she slipped into a coma and never woke up to see her husband's face again.

She had been his best friend for forty years and they had been married for twenty more.

Here I was, hearing all of this from a man sitting outside of the cancer hospital where he continued to get chemo treatments regularly to fight the cancer that was trying to take his life–a life that he felt torn to continue living without her.

When Bill's car came around the corner, he looked at it, looked back at me, and with tears in his eyes said, "That's her car. The last place we spent real time together. That's my Lola." I noticed her name in script lettering that ran along the side of the car.

"I'll keep my eyes open for you, Bill," I said, not knowing what else to say to this strong and wounded man. I hoped his treatments would be over soon and that they were helping. But if they weren't, I imagined he might like to be with his Lola again soon.

Every single person lives in a unique set of circumstances. The challenges I was facing and the cancer I was trying to survive were bigger than anything I'd ever faced before. It would have been easy to assume the person sitting next to me couldn't possibly have it as bad as I did at that point. But I don't want to be that person.

Bill reminded me that we're all going through things. If you have gone through things, you get it. If you haven't yet, you will. And when you do, always remember that you are not the only person surviving something. Everyone has.

15

be willing to forgive

Meet Mark.

Mark loves his dad, but he's usually angry with him. Mark always wanted to hang out with his dad and be more like him, but his dad had other priorities. Work was top, golf was up there, and the family was much farther down the list. Mark had grown up and grown through a lot of his emotions, yet he couldn't help but feel resentment every time he saw his dad playing and spending quality time with his youngest brother,

Michael, who certainly reaped the benefits of coming along fourteen years after Mark was grown.

That holiday was no exception. His dad and brother were out in the backyard playing catch. Granted, his dad didn't get around as well as he used to, but that was okay because his brother had pretty good aim.

"Sweetie, can you help me set the table?" his mom asked him. Mark nodded and grabbed enough plates for the houseful of people who were in random places doing God only knows what.

"I can see the envy in your eyes, Mark, she said quietly without really looking at him. We've been over this before. Your dad loves you. He always has. He just worked a lot. She paused. You can go on denying the time that is in front of you right now or you can hold it against him until he's gone." Mark never said a word. He was torn between anger and sadness hearing his mom talk.

The holiday came and went, and everyone traveled back to their homes. Mark couldn't shake what his mom had said.

He decided to write a letter to his dad. It had been a long time since he had sat down with a pen and paper in hand to write from his heart, but he knew his dad didn't have a lot of years left. Mark was a successful professional, a loving husband, and a great dad. It was time.

The first words were the hardest to write:

> Dad, I have some things I would like to share with you.

He paused. What now? He closed his eyes and his mind produced images of his dad walking in the door covered in dirt and sweat after a fifteen-hour day. He saw him jumping in the car with his buddies for a game of golf while Mark stood on the porch, just shy of his teen years, longing to go with him. A myriad of images crossed his mind before he landed on some that he had long forgotten.

He remembered his dad hugging his mom while kissing her neck. She laughed, pretending to push him away. He recalled prayers before family mealtime on Sunday nights, then the shadow of his dad walking into his room late at night, bending to hold his hands for a quick moment while whispering *God bless you.* Then there was the look of pride on his dad's face the day Mark graduated from law school, which he left without a penny in loans because his dad wrote the check every single year. The words started to flow.

> You've been a good father. I haven't ever told you that because I was too busy missing the things we *didn't* share, but I'm lucky to have a dad who has always loved me. You have taught me so many things over the years, like who I want to be and what is important in life. I can only imagine that you, too, have things you wish we had shared when I was younger, but I want you to know that I love you and I appreciate everything that you have sacrificed and done for me over the years.

Mark put down his pen. He quickly folded the letter, placed it in an addressed envelope, and drove to the nearest post office, in part because he was nervous he wouldn't send it if he waited, and in part because the clock was ticking and every minute that went by without sharing these words with his dad was another minute wasted. Once he dropped his letter in the mailbox outside, he sat in his car. A wash of relief, of release, swept through him. Tears rolled down his face, but for the first time, they were tears of happiness, of gratitude, of love for his father.

Forgiveness can be hard. But *not* forgiving is harder. Without it, we never know what we are missing, and in many ways, we poison ourselves with regret and anger. I hope you get the chance to feel a wash of relief like Mark experienced when he finally saw his dad through a different lens and stopped letting the past sabotage the time they had left. I hope the gift of forgiveness helps you live lighter and more freely. I've never met anyone who regretted forgiving someone. Seems like it might be worth a try.

16

get resourceful

I want to introduce you to my mom, JoEtta, and my aunt, Ava. They grew up close-ish in age. I have cherished black-and-white pictures of these sweet little girls for as long as I can remember. They are what sisterhood looks like to me.

They are also a couple of weirdos. (Please understand that if you call someone *weird* in my household, it's a compliment.) As I got older, I could see their differences more clearly and sometimes wondered what it was that kept them so close. The answer is *laughter*.

They are *those* women. The ones who start laughing at something and just can't stop without tears running down their cheeks. They laugh, and laugh, and laugh until it gets wonderfully awkward for everyone around them. These memories of their laughter are among my favorite childhood memories. I cherish them to this day.

There are a lot of stories of their belly laughs and tears, but this one might just be my favorite. It starts with something not-so-fun.

My grandma, Ethel, died of Acute Myeloid Leukemia when I was in high school. She had been a force throughout her entire life. In just about every memory, I have of her, she is wearing blue jeans, a tube top, and boots that resembled something like Uggs. Granted, the tube top sat lower and lower as she got older, but that didn't stop Grandma Ethel. She had short, spiky, cool hair. She rarely carried a purse. You were more likely to find her with her wallet tucked around her belt. Now that I think about it, she would have loved fanny packs!

When she died, her wish was to be cremated. But there weren't any instructions on what to do with her ashes.

So, when the funeral director handed over the small metal box containing the body that had been my grandma's, Aunt Ava took it–excuse me, took *her*–home.

For years, Ava kept Grandma on a windowsill so she could see outside, get fresh air, and…I don't know…bathe in the sun? Regardless, that metal box sat on that windowsill for years, until one day when my mom told Aunt Ava that she would be taking my brother to Florida and thought it seemed like a good time to scatter Grandma's remains there.

The sisters loaded up my brother, who was 18 at the time, my cousin (10), and um…Grandma Ethel. Then off they went.

They laughed their way from Indiana to Florida, having their usual adventures along the way while sharing stories of growing up with their mom. She had always loved the water, but she loved the sun even more. Her lifelong threat was to quit everything and become a beach bum who had daily swims with the dolphins and manatees. But never did it. Life kept her inland.

Once settled into their place near the ocean, the four (five) of them rented a pontoon and headed out to deeper waters. I wish I could tell you that at least one of the sisters really knew how to drive that pontoon, but neither of them did. You can probably imagine the winding, confusing course they took away from the marina into the waters, screaming at each other and laughing along the way. The younger two in the boat looked on with concern, wishing that Grandma was there to set everything straight.

They stumbled upon an inlet that felt right. Few homes could be seen. The water was fairly still. Trees lined the shore. It was the perfect place to lay their mom to rest.

"This is it," my mom said.

After a moment of silence, Ava reached for the tin can. They all looked at each other. Pontoon on the water. Touching moment. Tin can? Sealed. No can opener.

They all started looking around the rented pontoon for anything that might help them break the seal.

"Wait a minute!" Aunt Ava shouted as she started digging into her bag. "I have a..."

To hear my mom tell the story, Aunt Ava pulled out a combat knife as if she was ready to go to battle.

To hear Aunt Ava tell the story, it was a simple pocket knife she always carried because she is resourceful.

No matter the size of the knife, Aunt Ava began jabbing at the top of the can. *Shunk! Shunk! Shunk!* Just enough to sprinkle out a few ashes.

Then, *Shunkkkkkkkkk!* The knife went through the other side of the can and both the knife and the can fell to the boat's floor.

My brother was at the wheel, trying to hold the pontoon steady from the winds that had started picking up. The boat had a sway to it. Holding steady-ish. Then? Gust of wind. Rolling can. Grandma's ashes peppering the floor of the boat. Laughing sisters.

My cousin jumped to her feet on her seat and started screaming, "You're spilling Grandma!!!" while the sisters tried to find their way to the can through tears of laughter.

Once recovered, they took what was left of my sweet grandma's ashes and ceremonially lifted the can into the air. What else could possibly go wrong? Oh, I'll tell you.

The wind. It shifted. Now the pontoon floor wasn't the only thing wearing Grandma's ashes. As their collective tears merged into sadness and disgust (mixed with continued laughter) they saw movement in the water. A manatee surfaced. Her sweet little nostrils caused ripples in the water. Her body glided across the top of the ocean and they could see every detail of her. She slowly started to make her way back under the water, and a shadow appeared. Then my family got a glimpse of that mama's sweet little baby trailing alongside her.

Grandma would have loved this moment. Shoot. Grandma *was* this moment.

Ava tucked the knife back into her bag and my mom gave her a smile of thanks, knowing what they would have missed if her sister wasn't resourceful.

"She's definitely here," one of them said. And with that, they turned to face the wind, leaving Grandma behind to swim with the manatees.

17

get weird

Journal Entry — March 24, 2020

Let's talk about my fuzzy head, faith over fear, yesterday's trip to the hospital, and a deep conversation with the echocardiogram tech while lying half-naked on the table.

My hair is starting to grow back…sort of. There is going to be no graceful way for it to grow, so I've decided to make the most of this COVID lockdown time and let it do what it's going to do. I still don't have to shave. My eyelashes and eyebrows keep trying to grow in, then just fall out.

I know I'm not alone. Any woman who has had her lashes done is going through her own mourning period every time one of those beautiful, lush lashes floats from her face to the bathroom sink. I feel your pain, sister. The biggest difference is that I didn't pay for mine.

There are a lot of words that I would use to describe how I am feeling during this time - personally, from a community perspective, as a nation, and as part of our world, but *fear* is not a constant. I am cautious. I am aware. I even have moments when I get a little anxious, but overall, I'm not afraid.

I don't believe that fear comes from God. Allow me to go really deep for a moment, fear is a tool used effectively and powerfully by forces that have nothing to do with God. That, my friends, is a conversation for another time. Just know that I'm okay if you think I'm crazy for writing those words. I'm okay if you feel confused or even taken aback. You can feel any way you want about me and what I just put out there.

Regardless, I would ask you to do one simple thing the next time you feel afraid. Give that fear to God. It's okay if you don't know Him very well. He knows you. It's also okay if you know Him so well that you've got a "What's up, *G*?" kind of relationship with Him. (Actually, I don't think I would call him *G*, but to each their own.) If you just tell God that you're afraid, my experience tells me that you'll invite His peace, and the moments that come afterward create the opportunity to lean into something greater, more productive, and surprisingly more powerful than fear.

Yesterday, I went to the hospital for a scheduled trip for a routine heart test, as well as my targeted inhibitor and to get mapped for radiation. It was like a ghost town there. After the initial screening at the door and the questions that I can now recite in my sleep… "Have you been out of the country in the last 14…" and so forth, they took me back and got me settled in.

I closed my eyes and heard the familiar sounds–nurses talking, papers rustling, the mini fridge humming. Someone not too far away was watching tv, and though I couldn't figure out what they were watching, every once in a while, I heard the person giggling. If I'd had the energy, I would have joined them. The warm blankets brought to me by the aids were hugging me when no one else could touch me and I felt at home. Here I sat, surrounded by people who are sick, many of whom won't last in this world much longer, but there was laughter and comfort. For an hour, our bizarre reality felt comfortable. Even normal.

Because my inhibitor can affect the heart, I have an echocardiogram every three months. It's a check-in to make sure my heart is still doing well. It's super easy, but this one was special, interesting, and even a little weird. (To be fair, I started the weirdness.) I was wearing the typical blue hospital gown on the top, open in the front, with my comfy yoga pants and socks on the bottom.

When the tech walked in, I said, "When people lie down on their backs like this, do their feet go out to the side like mine?" I pointed to my feet, looking like they were in an argument and had turned their little feet backs on each other. "Or do they point straight up at the ceiling?"

He paused. He seemed to really be thinking about it. "I don't know," he replied with hesitation and curiosity. "I'll have to pay attention."

I looked it up. I am something called *duck-footed* and should really give it some attention. This will go on my least-of-my-concerns list for now.

After that, it was *game on*. We talked about books, his education, the fact that getting an echocardiogram is reminiscent of getting an ultrasound when you are pregnant. The gel is cold, the wand rolling over your skin, the sound of words being typed on the keyboard, watching the tech's face to see if he sees anything concerning. If he had printed me a snapshot of my heart like those I used to get of my babies, I would have shared it with my family and posted it on my refrigerator.

As we were coming to a close, I said, "I feel like I'm supposed to share something with you, but it's gonna get strange."

I need you, my friend, to picture this. I have a baldish-fuzzy head. I'm all marked up with *Xs* on my body in preparation for radiation. (Seriously, I look like a child got a hold of a Sharpie and wrote all over her Barbie.) I'm wearing a medical mask. I have nothing on from the waist up. And, as he is sitting next to me finalizing his report, I started telling him about some changes Jeff and I have made in our household.

We are tithing 10% off the top of our income. I told him that I have wanted to do this for years and although I never used to understand *why*, as Christians, we're instructed to do this, I felt called to start. Then Jeff came home last fall and told me that he wanted to do it, too. So I immediately said *yes* and we started tithing. But then I got my second diagnosis. And the medical bills started piling up…again.

We stayed true to our commitment and, just as God promises when we obey, He blessed us in ways we didn't ask for or expect. I shared with this young man the many meals, gift cards, and kindness that so many have shown us. I told him about all the offers to pick up groceries. There are things that I can't share with you here that would blow your mind but trust me when I tell you that God is good, and He keeps His word on everything. We are so grateful. And I told my tech all of this.

That sweet young eco tech opened up about his faith and shared that he is a practicing Jehovah's Witness. We talked about how he has a lot of stereotypes to overcome–his religion, the color of his skin, and the fact that he is a millennial man. But overall, he told me that he just wants to love people through their similarities and their differences. He doesn't want to judge. He doesn't want to debate. He just wants to love people.

While I *wanted* to jump up and tackle him with a hug and a resounding, "Yes!" I managed to lie still and calmly reply, "Me too." Then the annoying phone rang and interrupted our make-shift therapy session. His next appointment was in the waiting room. He hung up the phone and stepped out so I could get dressed.

When he opened the door to walk me back out, he said, "I'm sad that you have to go."

I was, too. At a time when we aren't supposed to be closer than six feet away from each other, we instinctively hugged as I was leaving.

Imagine if we all took a moment to say the things that we think and feel without fear of judgment, without debate, without offense or defense. It'd be weird but it'd be wonderful. Our conversations would go to places we haven't explored. And, in the end, we'd probably laugh a bit harder and love a bit deeper. I like the idea of both.

This strange pandemic is hard, I know. We're losing people that we love. It hurts. We don't know the right thing to do. It's confusing. But I'm trying to think of it like a time-out. Sometimes we need to be put in time-out so we can meditate, play games, communicate with people in different time zones and those who live in our own homes. We can write letters and journal. We can connect in ways we can't in our normal busy lives. For all of that, I say "YES!"

The world is weird right now. Might as well embrace it. Get out there! Start a conversation. Get deep. Get real. Or just sit still. But above all, get weird. And while you're at it, lie down and check out your feet because apparently, this duck-footed thing can put additional stress on your joints and ligaments. And nobody needs that.

18

people will judge you

With 100% certainty, I tell you that people will judge you. It's not right on any level, but it is something that most of the world's population must actively fight against. A lot of people don't have the fight in them, for whatever reason. When they're young, when they're old, or somewhere in between, people judge.

Just like you, I've been judged for a lot of things. Funny enough, it usually has to do with my hair. In fairness, I've made some questionable choices over the years. I've been bald (not a choice, but a reality). I've forgotten what my natural color was because of all of the bleach. And for a long time, I had a blonde…um…stripe? No. It was a streak. Somehow that sounds less trashy, I think.

I'm big on showing up as your true self rather than trying to fit in. This goes for both my personal life and my professional life. I'm not going to try to hide who I am for anyone. So, when I got invited to join a local leadership group in Indianapolis that took in a new class of leaders every year, I accepted. I…me…the one with the streak in my hair, accepted, as did about ten other professionals.

It was exciting to join this group and to know that I was going to grow, learn about our city and state, about philanthropy and general leadership approaches, and gain skills for building a community of leaders to impact our city and beyond. I was also excited to learn from my classmates, knowing that we would be meeting a couple of days each month for the next year and that we would build relationships we didn't even know we wanted.

We did personality testing. Cool. Love that stuff. We acted out scenarios and had to watch back the recordings, critiquing ourselves and our classmates. Torture. Pure torture.

We studied Shackleton. Yummy. So attractive in so many ways. I mean, Shackleton was an Irish explorer who led several expeditions. Arguably, his most proclaimed adventure was to travel on a ship called *Endurance* to Antarctica in the early 1900s, where they would attempt to become the first people to ever cross the ice-covered continent.

But instead, my boyfriend Shackleton and his crew of 27 men watched from their camp as their abandoned ship was seized by the freezing waters and slowly crushed by ice over the course of months. They were trapped at their camp, which was on a floating piece of ice, with no resources, low morale, and the hovering fear that they would never see their homes or families again. There's much more to their experience but, in short, Shackleton miraculously led his entire crew home, without a ship and without serious harm. Shackleton is often studied and considered by many to be one of the best leaders of all time. He made some questionable choices personally, but I forgive him.

Our class broke into teams of two to discuss his leadership style. I got paired up with Deonte. Deonte seemed cool and appeared to be laid back. He was an attractive guy, a bit younger than I was, married with two small young children. Deonte was a professional in the banking industry and while we hadn't had the chance to have any big conversation up to this point, I felt pretty confident that if I needed anything, Deonte would be the kind of person who would help.

He and I went into a small business office in the building, opened our notebooks, and began to address the questions provided for each team to work through. We only had an hour together, but with about ten minutes to spare, Deonte closed his notebook and stared at me.

"What's up?" I asked.

"I've got to come clean with you," he said with some hesitation. "I actually feel kind of bad. You see, when you walked into the room on that first day, I found myself wondering how in the world anyone could let you run an organization."

I don't know what sound came out of my mouth but imagine that a sigh and a growl had a baby. That's the noise I made.

"I know," he said. "Not cool. But now I get it. I really get it."

Thanks, Deonte. Drop a bomb like that just before our time is up.

The next month, when I saw Deonte, I pulled him aside. I wanted to know what it was that made him question my professionalism and abilities.

His answer was easy. It had everything to do with my appearance. It was the tattoos. It was the eclectic and non-businessy way that I dressed. It was the jewelry. And, you guessed it, the hair.

No matter how wrong it is to judge people, sometimes people will be correct in their opinion of you. But sometimes, they will be wrong.

Don't base your life–your actions, your attitude, your core values, your purpose, your faith, or even your hair–on who people think you are. You do you. Let people be confused and beautifully surprised if they make the effort to figure out who you really are.

Wouldn't Deonte freak out if he saw my current mohawk, or if he found out my plan for getting another tattoo later this month? It's okay, Deonte. I still think you're cool. As for Shackleton, don't worry, my husband is well aware that I have a crush on an Irish explorer who died in 1922. Everything is fine.

19

keep showing up

I should probably clarify…keep showing up *when you're invited and welcomed.* If you're not invited or welcomed, things get kind of odd, and not in a good way.

Recently, I went *next level* making sure a lifetime of captured memories will be accessible forever. I sought out a local company to take random bits and put them all on one hard drive. It was not cheap and yet, it was worth every penny. Some of those memories had not been unlocked since they were recorded.

These days, memories you can touch come in all kinds of forms. I have negatives from Jeff and my wedding, and from when our oldest was a baby. There are about five different-sized tapes from the five different video cameras we had when the kids were little. There are scrapbooks that cover parts and pieces of the last couple of decades and are adorned with faded stickers and handwritten notes detailing dates and highlighting words of encouragement. There are flash drives with Lord-only-knows-what on them, hard drives, and enough printed pictures to fill up a small walk-in closet. (I know this because the printed pictures actually fill up my small walk-in closet.)

It took me weeks to go through all of the old things that suddenly felt new again. Newborns and toddlers, dogs and cats, houses, birthdays, and holidays. My husband, who clearly doesn't age, was in all of them. My kids went from rolling over to running to living their lives as young adults. My mom and her husband were there for each meaningful moment. My sister, my brothers, and a few of my most cherished friends were woven throughout all of it, bringing the structure of our village to life.

One of the constants that I kept seeing in this massive collection of memories was The Aunties. It seemed that every new video that came on my screen included the two of them. These are two of my very best friends in the whole world.

Auntie #1 was the first person I met in college. She was painfully introverted and yet, she was on the Ball State University Welcome Team for my dorm. My mom and Joe (see…they were a constant) had just left and my roommate hadn't arrived yet. I sat on my dorm room floor, hesitantly opening taped-up cardboard boxes, trying not to cry because I felt so alone and scared for this new part of life. But then I heard someone at my dorm room door. There I sat, feeling so small on the floor. And there she stood, superhero-like in the doorframe. I felt safe and seen as soon as we started talking. When she walked away, I knew we'd be friends. And we were. We had so much fun in the years that followed her kind introduction that day.

After college, I got to know Auntie #1's best friend (Auntie #2). A group of us ran around together, riding that fine line between having fun and trying to not get into too much trouble. As we got older, we'd run into each other at bookstores and restaurants, and we always found ways to spend quality time together. We invited each other to housewarming parties and other celebrations. I knew that both Aunties and I would be friends for a long time.

Auntie #2 became the second person I hired at Joy's House, and since there were only three of us in the beginning, we worked together closely for years. By *closely*, I mean that there was a time when my cats were temporarily living on the second floor at Joy's House and she helped feed them on a daily basis. By *closely*, I mean that I walked the journey of her father's failing health with her and simultaneously fell in love with her family. By *closely*, I mean that during a season when I was taking my newborn to work with me, I would hand my baby off to Auntie #2 so that I could go into a meeting. Without a doubt, I knew we would be connected forever.

Kids. Deaths. Marriages. Homes. Dogs. Life. The Aunties and I have done it all together. The memories I'd gathered only tell part of the story. There are funny parts of the story, like the time the Aunties were sitting on the couch with Maia and Webster, posing for one of these photos, and Web was only a few years old, crying uncontrollably, throwing a fit. Like the-fit-of-a-lifetime. Maia was screaming and clearly would have rather been doing anything else. Yet Auntie #2 sat facing the camera, eyes as wide as they would go, while

Auntie #1 had her head turned looking at Auntie #2 with a look that said, *I'm extremely concerned about this situation. How do we get out of this place?!* It's a classic picture.

Then there's the night Auntie #1, Auntie #2, Jeff, and I went out to enjoy sushi and time with each other, and the server arrived with a back-up server who also had a back-up server just so they could deliver our feast. That's how we knew that *maybe* we had ordered too much. That meal turned into what felt like a sushi-eating contest. We polished off every single bit of food on our table. Maybe we should have been embarrassed, but instead, we were just really full.

When The Aunties got married years ago and I got to stand up as a Matron of Honor with them. It was truly *my honor*. I got the chance to show up for them the way they had been showing up for me, and so many others. For a myriad of reasons, I will forever cherish the pictures I saved of them standing in front of so many people who love and support them.

New Year's celebrations. Our dogs growing up together. Moves to other states and back again. New homes for our families. Aging parents. Illnesses. Surgeries. Scares. Reunited family members. Shaving our heads before chemo caused my hair to fall out. (Yep. They shaved their heads, too). We've done it all together.

Because of the ways we've kept showing up for each other over the years, The Aunties are more than friends. They are family. That's why my kids know them as The Aunties. And I have every confidence that we'll keep showing up for each other until our last days in this world.

Seeing The Aunties scattered across my adult life brought me to a realization that one of the best things we can do for the people we love is to keep showing up. Hard times will come. Uncomfortable times will come. Times will come when we don't know what to say or do once we get there, but the simple fact that we *keep showing up* ties us together.

20

if you bring a problem, bring a solution

Anna had been watching the weather for weeks in preparation for her upcoming outdoor wedding and reception. She and her fiancé, Corey, would sit on the couch and consult Weather Bug, local forecasts, and the trusted Farmer's Almanac. She was not messing around.

As the weeks passed by, other priorities crept into her space like flower delivery times and the arrival of family. Clouds rolled in and out during that time and she watched with a hopeful eye.

Friday arrived. Anna and her mom ran all of the errands. The back of the car was packed with Costco-sized boxes full of food when they pulled up at the family apple orchard just a short time before the casual rehearsal dinner they were hosting on-site. Instantly, Anna could see her 3-year-old self running around the yard, playing tag, and laughing with her sister. She remembered long days picking apples with her grandfather and hearing stories of his childhood when he spent long days picking apples with his parents. She closed her eyes and listened to the trees blowing in the wind and could feel a calmness come over her.

She was snapped back to reality by the squeal of family members pouring out of the house. She felt the love as they raced toward her. *It's happening! You're getting married! What can we carry for you?* She returned the sentiments with a bit of shyness at being the center of attention and before she knew it, everything was unpacked and the tent that stood waiting to host their meal was full of people.

Anna took a few minutes inside the house to get herself together for the gathering. It didn't take much. She was naturally lovely. She may not have ever known it, but everyone around her sure did.

The rehearsal went as planned. Dinner was ready as planned. The welcome speeches and conversations about Anna and Corey were better than planned. The rain, however, was not planned, nor was it welcomed. It rained big raindrops. It rained little raindrops. It rained *all of the raindrops.*

"Uh oh!" They heard someone say from the back of the tent. "We have standing water."

That standing water turned into running water and before they could do anything to even try to stop it, they were all standing in a very large puddle of apple orchard water. There was nothing they could do except say their goodbyes for the night and pray for sunshine in the morning.

Morning came but it didn't bring sunshine. Anna, her mom, and her bridesmaids all met at the salon for hair and makeup. They were in good, prewedding, very-wet-day-outside moods when Anna's phone dinged. It was a picture of Corey standing at the wedding site with water up to the top of his boots, and a message that read: "How's it going? Don't worry. We've got this. Enjoy your time today. Love you."

Anna closed her eyes again. She took a deep breath. *It will be fine. It will be fine.*

Soon, her phone rang. "Anna, we're probably not going to be able to have the reception at the orchard..." her family member trailed off. Then she confidently added, "Do you trust us?"

"I do," Anna said. She hung up, looked at her wedding crew, and told them there was a problem, but there was also a solution.

"What are they going to do?" one of them asked.

"I'm not sure," she answered, as she smiled a sweet smile and then turned back to the mirror to finish getting ready.

My family and I arrived shortly before the ceremony was set to begin. We were greeted by a bridge made of scrap wood that the family had pulled from the barn. Hay, which was gathered from a friendly neighbor, had been laid out around the wedding site to help soak up the massive amounts of water flooding that area of the orchard–an area that Anna's grandfather said had never flooded in five generations.

We were seated just in time for the ceremony to begin. The music started playing. We all stood. I glanced at the groom and saw his face light up, then he started to smile. Around the corner came the bridesmaids, cautiously making their way across the makeshift bridge toward the Wedding Tree, which the couple had chosen as their ceremony spot months earlier when they got engaged. The bridesmaids were adorable, each carrying flowers, hair perfectly placed, and dressed in her wedding attire...and brand-new rain boots.

Last in this line of beauties was Anna, sporting rain boots, adorned with bright blue, green, and purple flowers, that peeked out below the hem of her wedding gown with each step. She was escorted by her father, who was cautiously holding his daughter's hand while surrounded by her bridesmaids, carrying umbrellas, just in case. As unique as these moments were leading up to the ceremony, there was still one surprise left. A gust of wind came through the aisle, just as Anna was reaching for Corey's hand to take her place by the Wedding Tree and blew her dress up. All the way up. Yes. The bride had just flashed her wedding guests.

With grace and sweetness, she turned to those of us gathered and said, "You're welcome." She and Corey burst into laughter, which gave the rest of us permission to laugh, too. Suddenly, instantly, any concern or tension that might have tried to creep in as a result of the storm melted away.

Little did we know that, while we were witnessing this couple's marriage ceremony, a reception was being created down the road. As instructed at the close of the ceremony, we all found our way to the local church and, like magic, walked in to find the cake (which was actually a delicious-looking donut tower) in its proper place. The food was hot and ready. The decorations were perfect. The newlyweds never had to worry about a thing. With a lot of love and a dry roof over our heads, we celebrated the happy couple and their new life together.

I loved this day so much. This lesson is one that most of us can learn from because it is much easier to identify a problem than it is to solve it. Problems are usually obvious, but solutions take time and intention. Solutions ease anxiety and angst. Coming with a solution keeps problems from taking over otherwise great days, whether special occasions, work challenges, or everyday setbacks.

If you ask Anna about her wedding day, she will tell you that it was the best day. People just did what needed to be done and worked together so that no one person, or in this case, no one couple, had to stress over any of the issues at hand. Her initial plan for the wedding was good, but the collective solution made her wedding day perfect in ways she could have never imagined.

Imagine if Anna had been sitting with her hair in curlers, scrambling to come up with a Plan B. Or imagine if Corey had just stood in that tent with the water moving around him stewing about how the day was surely ruined. Imagine if the family had sat around a table talking about all of the things that were going wrong. What a different experience their wedding would have turned out to be.

But not this family. Not on this special day. Instead, they jumped into action and saved the day, donut tower and all. It's an example we can all stand to remember the next time a problem pops up and we're tempted to throw in the towel.

Every problem life throws at us presents an opportunity to come up with a solution. And so often, these opportunities hold magic that we would never discover if we didn't have a problem in the first place.

21

some people will leave your life

People come into our lives for a lot of reasons. They also leave for a lot of reasons.

They physically move away. They emotionally go away. Sometimes, they leave and come back. Sometimes, they leave forever. A lot of times, we don't understand why unless they tell us. Or they tell us and we still don't understand. Bottom line...people will leave your life. This I can guarantee.

I work with family caregivers who are caring for loved ones whose lives have been altered by a diagnosis– sometimes physical, sometimes mental, and sometimes both. A lot of people leave their lives at this point, and we often work with caregivers to help them process the changes taking place in their lives.

Ginger was one of these caregivers. She had been the primary caregiver for her mother for the previous three years. Ginger was undeniably tired and showing signs of depression, so I asked her if we could sit down and talk.

"What's going on with you?" I asked.

"I just feel so alone," she said, looking down at her hands, which were clenched together and resting in her lap.

I responded, "I'm here for you."

"I know, and I appreciate that. It's my friends [leaving] that bother me the most. I guess I should say my old friends because I don't really feel like we know each other anymore."

She went on to explain that during the first two years, her friends rallied around her. They formed teams to participate in walks for people, like her mom, living with the aftereffects of strokes. They brought meals and asked what they could pick up at the grocery when they were there. Her friends even helped clean the house and take care of the yard.

They also invited her to do normal things as they had always done, like having coffee together and hosting book clubs. Ginger attended as often as she could, but her mom's care took priority. By the third year, she felt like her friends were dropping off one by one, and she couldn't figure out anything she had done wrong. She felt as if they had just given up inviting her because so much of her time and attention was devoted to her mom. That reality made her sad.

I shared with her that this is normal. It's normal in life for relationships to change. Caregiving is no different. Some people will leave our lives and it's not always about us.

Over the years at Joy's House, we have observed friends, family members, and acquaintances leaving people because:

- Staying and caring means opening their old emotional wounds and it's just too hard.
- They don't know what to say.
- They are envious of attention and love.
- They are afraid or uncomfortable.
- They have different values.
- They simply don't want to be involved anymore.
- They only know how to get *so close.*
- Seeing what a caregiver is going through scares them and makes them think about the people in their lives and all of the *what-ifs.*

The fact is, even if you've never found yourself in the role of caregiver, people will still leave your life. They'll pass away, they'll move to another area, they'll make excuses for why they can't do things with you, or they'll stop returning your calls.

One thing is certain. Circumstances and people change over the years, but nothing can take away the time you had together. The years and moments you had those relationships can remain as important, memorable, and influential as they have ever been...if you let them.

Embrace the people in your life today. But if they leave, be thankful for the opportunity you had to love them and learn alongside them. When someone leaves, perhaps space is being created for relationships that are more aligned with where you are in life now. Don't waste your energy trying to recreate the past. Move forward with gratitude for everyone who has been, is currently, or ever will be there for you.

22

sometimes the best thing to do is shut your mouth

There isn't anything more to say about this one, so I will stop talking now.

23

you are beautiful

Journal Entry — November 18, 2019

This last week has brought some waiting. I've been waiting for physical wounds to heal, waiting for doctor appointments to arrive, waiting for pathology results, and for my mid-day nap. I've found that it's always a bit strange to have limited functionality combined with time on my hands. One of the things I've been doing to fill this space is going through old photos–albums, on my phone, photos on my computer, and on various disks, flash drives, and tapes to see when I stopped printing pictures so I can make that right.

It's amazing to me how many memories are influenced by the pictures that we've taken. Holidays came to life as I flipped through photos of Mom and Dad Tom together, all of us gathered together, opening Christmas presents, filling the holiday with church, and food, and eventually, poker with my aunts, uncles, cousins, with our matriarch, Grandma Ethel.

When I was in high school, I remember shopping at Merry-Go-Round (think leopard-print tops and acid-washed jeans) with Grandma once, thinking I was going to leave with a new wardrobe. I got a simple pair of shorts. Grandma, however, got a kick-ass metal belt with spikes. If she had been someone else's grandma, I would have wished she was mine.

She collected injured animals and neglected people like it was her job. We hand-raised two abandoned baby squirrels that would play in my Fisher-Price playhouse, and when we rang the doorbell, they would peek their heads out the little windows like we were arriving for a dinner party, and they couldn't wait for us to come in. My grandma did the same with people. If someone needed a place to land, she opened her door to them.

She always made candles at the high-top table near the kitchen and dried fruit in the hallway pantry. She influenced my life more than she will ever realize. And though she has been gone since I was in high school, I still miss her.

Back to my photo project. I fast-forwarded through what felt like thousands of softball games, the birth of my siblings, hours of Pac-Man and Kaboom, hockey, hockey, more hockey, sleepovers, riding bikes in the neighborhood, and playing tag while waiting for the school bus to arrive. Then I landed on pictures from high school.

Keep in mind that I am currently the parent of a high school senior. When we started planning Maia's senior pictures, I told her that I wanted to join her in the beginning, then I would leave so that she could have some freedom with the photo shoot. She seemed to appreciate that. But I got this cancer diagnosis that week, which changed everything. As she was walking out the front door to go to the shoot, she asked, "Mom, do you want to come with me?"

Yes! I nearly sprinted to the car before she could change her mind.

Witnessing the taking of senior pictures was really like being on the set of a modeling shoot. I saw my girl in new ways. She was breathtaking, fun, charismatic…beautiful. I knew all of these things about her, but on this day I saw them at a new level.

When we got her pictures back, I shared them. And as I was going through these old photos, I shared one of my senior pictures which, by the way, was not taken at a cool photo shoot. It was a shot of me sitting side-saddle in the grass in front of a wagon wheel with a *very moving* expression on my face. Let me tell you, it was a realllllly sexy shot. (And by that, I mean it was *not at all* a really sexy shot.)

I don't live for thumbs up or comments on social media, but something important happened when I shared her photo and then mine. You see, I read back through my high school diaries, which by the way, will not be shared anywhere, ever. (They should be burned in some kind of cleansing ritual and never read again.) But as I look back at who I was in high school–and even into adulthood–I never felt pretty. But looking at those pictures and seeing so many kind comments, I realize that I was beautiful.

Isn't it funny how we can see beauty in everyone around us, but not in ourselves? I see it in nearly every child I meet. I see it at Joy's House with every adult who comes to spend their days with us. Beauty isn't based on size, hair, or how big our eyes are. It runs so much deeper than *pretty*.

With that, I owe my 16-year-old self an apology. I'm sorry. I know who I am *not* and I see who I was back then. I'm not ever going to consider myself the prettiest girl in the room. As a matter of fact, I don't want to be. I know a lot of really pretty people and there seems to be a lot of pressure that comes with being pretty.

Now I realize that, if I was ever forced to choose between being *pretty* and being *beautiful*, I know without a doubt that I'd choose *beautiful*.

24

accept support

It would be impossible for me to guess how many times I've told family caregivers that they must learn how to accept support. It's how people show love and care. When you are going through something major in life, good or hard, people want to show up. When it's the hard stuff, we don't always know how to go about it or what to say. The offer often goes something like this…

Other person: "Is there anything you need?"

Person going through hard stuff: "No."

Other person: "Okay, well, anything at all that I can do…just let me know."

It's a statement that's meant to be wide open so that if anything is needed, we'll be notified. However, it's *so big* that the other person doesn't always know what is reasonable to ask for. The offer usually remains unaccepted. Neither person wins.

When we lost three babies, people didn't know what to do. I would get so strange about flowers because they were beautiful for a few days and then they were gone, which felt like an unfortunate metaphor for my babies being gone, too. I wish I had learned sooner to say yes when someone asked me to meet them for coffee or offered to just come over and hang out during that period in my life. I could have used that.

I'm sure I had my reasons for not accepting, but I'm sorry to say that one of them is that I was trying to be strong, and instead of being vulnerable with my feelings. I pushed through and pushed on. I've heard it said that often people don't accept support because they're afraid others will see them as weak. I likely fell into that category. Truth is, I *was* weak. I *was* sad. I *was* broken in many ways. I should have accepted the support.

I did learn from those experiences though, so that's something. I have had to learn to accept support. Throughout the last dozen or so years, with all of the medical issues Jeff and I have had, we've built a tribe and have been overwhelmed by the most beautiful support I could have ever imagined. We've been blessed by meals that were life-giving. And, let me tell you, we've also ended up with some pretty suspect casseroles. So. Many. Casseroles.

On the other hand, we've received a meal chain where we *were* specific…light on the chicken, no pasta, high protein, please deliver between 3:00 and 5:00 pm. If the porch light is on, please place the meal in the cooler.

Take a guess on which experience the people making dinners liked best. You nailed it if you guessed the last one where we asked for what we actually wanted. They liked it, and we did, too.

I never grew tired of the random cards that found their way to our mailbox and the beautiful words that people would write inside. I never grew tired of the prayers.

There were some incredibly generous gifts that blew our minds, like the time some of my high school guy friends pooled together money and sent Jeff and me on a date in our own city, complete with an overnight stay downtown. We desperately needed that time together and I hope those idiotic-boys-who-turned-into-incredible-men know how much that kindness meant to us.

Another time, someone paid a month of our mortgage. In some ways, I was embarrassed to accept that one, but with medical bills piling up, it was the gift we couldn't see coming but appreciated immensely.

Maia's softball team all wore pink socks and decorated the dugout to show me their love. I still get teary when I think about walking up to see those sweet young girls on the field in a sea of pink. Some of the parents dressed in pink, too. And the son of a friend of mine changed his shoelaces to pink and said he was going to wear them until *Mrs. McIntosh got better*.

Web's classmates all made me cards. They said things like, "When I am sick, my mom makes me eat soup. Eat your soup." Another read, "Web will be okay." Another read, "You're a good dad." (I have no idea…it was the thought that counted.)

My YaYas (my high school best friends) all wore pink for me when I couldn't join them for a weekend together. Friends who lived nearby drove me around, joined me at chemo, checked on me consistently, and made sure the kids were getting to school, to practices, and out for adventures with them.

My sorority sisters and other college friends came together for a night of nothing but love and gifts before I started chemo. My mom was here every time, for all of it. My mother-in-law did anything we needed.

When Jeff was sick with kidney cancer, everyone did it all over. And again for his leukemia. And again for my last breast cancer.

I said it before and I'll say it again, I can't imagine how hard it has been for people to keep loving us and supporting us through all of this. It has to be exhausting. But somehow, they do.

We are blessed with love and care even though it might have taken us ten years to figure it out. Now I can say that accepting support from others has changed our lives for the better.

Most of us would rather be the one without the needs. But take it from someone with a lot of needs that I didn't choose, learning to receive kindness has been a beautiful and humbling experience. And necessary. Because we really do need other people.

25

be the strength for someone else

Ricky had been an outsider ever since he was a little boy. His parents were odd by most standards and had some pretty major issues of their own. Ricky was that kid who waited at the bus stop in silence and didn't dare try to engage with anyone. He was always first in line, sat in the front of the bus, and was the first one off as soon as the bus arrived at school. He went straight to class and never looked forward to seeing a friend...mainly because he didn't have one.

He hurt inside, but never cried a tear in front of anyone. He was afraid that if he did, the others would attack like desperate lions suffering a famine. Those days nearly killed him.

Ricky made fine grades and never caused a problem for any of his teachers. He was never late for an appointment. But he will also never look back on high school with fond memories. He isn't going to accidentally stumble upon his prom pictures or his superlatives or his letter jacket and remember the good old days. He doesn't have any of those.

He would, however, remember one particular Tuesday in April when a couple of the high school jerks were walking behind him in the hall on the way to class. You know the guys. *Those guys.* They weren't doing anything horrible in the sense that they weren't touching him, throwing anything, or harming him physically, but they were beating him up mentally. In nearly a whisper, they were directing nasty comments at Ricky.

"Freak."

"Nobody likes you."

"Man, what's wrong with you?"

He just wanted them to stop talking.

"You gonna cry? Huh? What a waste…"

Ricky kept walking straight ahead, trying to get to class, or hoping to run into a teacher, or wishing he could disappear into a cloud of smoke.

The long hallway felt like it was getting longer and longer.

Ricky looked down the row of lockers, praying for the guys to stop taunting him. Then Dan turned the corner up ahead and began walking toward them. Dan was athletic, but not a super jock. He was good-looking, but not the homecoming king. He was well-liked, but not class president. He was a normal guy.

The next few moments were blurry for Ricky. No words were spoken. Dan stared down the jerks and the jerks somehow got broader shoulders. The silence that hung in the air felt heavy and scary to Ricky. Then Dan, whom Ricky knew only from a distance, made a move.

As Ricky and the collection of jerks approached Dan, he turned around and started walking with them. Without a word, he walked close to Ricky and even closer to the jerks. No one said anything and no one needed to. Dan's presence provided a wall of protection between Ricky and the jerks.

Ricky not only made it to class that day, but he also made it through high school. Something changed for him that day. No one ever picked on him again in that way. Dan changed Rickey's life when he stopped walking away and started walking with Ricky.

When Dan and Ricky ran into each other years later, Dan couldn't help but smile at the man before him. They were decades older now. Like, grandchildren-who-are-out-of-college older. After the usual niceties and haven't-seen-you-in-awhile exchanges, Ricky kind of leaned in and said, "You know, Dan, when we were younger, you were the only person who was ever nice to me."

Ricky extended his right hand. The two men shook hands and said goodbye. And Ricky turned around and started walking away, hand-in-hand with his wife, and happy.

High school. Whether it was five days or five decades ago, high school always seems like yesterday and a lifetime ago all at the same time. And when you think back about it all, remember the guy who got picked on all of the time? Or the girl with the crooked glasses who broke out in a sweat if she accidentally looked someone in the eye?

Was it *you*?

If it *was* you, I hope someone stood up for you. If no one did, I'm so sorry. I hope you've somehow learned that you didn't deserve that.

If I *wasn't* you, I hope you did what you could do to support or empower or protect that kid. And I hope you run into those people years later so they can let you know how profoundly you helped them survive whatever they were going through. If they never get the chance to tell you, remember Ricky and know that you made a difference.

It's easy to *think* about doing the right thing. But it's another thing to confront our pride, or fear, or distractions, and step up when someone needs to borrow a little of our strength. Everything we do–and everything we *don't* do–can impact people more than we might realize.

It doesn't take much to show kindness to someone. It might not require a single word. Just know that your actions have the power to change someone's life. And, for those who know what it feels like to be that kid, it is a powerful thing to learn to be the person you needed back then.

26

it's okay to fail

When I think about failing at something, I think about writing this book. I've been talking about it, making notes, and thinking about the *what-ifs* for more than a dozen years. I've got lots of files and trays full of Post-it notes and handwritten messages. But for more than a dozen years, I failed to write it.

There are some really good excuses I could give for not writing it before now. I mean, really, between Jeff's health and mine, raising kids, family challenges, Joy's House, oh...a global pandemic.

But the true reason is…I was afraid. I was scared that you would never read these words. Worse yet, I was afraid that you *would* read them and find them silly and unrelatable, or that you wouldn't like me anymore.

What hit me recently is how, by *not* writing this book, I was already failing. And according to my own life mantra, I either needed to do something about it or stop talking about it.

Life is unpredictable. I see this every day with our Guests at Joy's House. One day someone was a successful musician, and the next day he couldn't remember how to read the notes. Another used to run marathons on a regular basis, then suddenly she couldn't walk from the chair to the kitchen without assistance because her legs didn't work. Life *is* unpredictable and it's precious.

Eleanor Roosevelt is credited with saying, "What would you do if you knew you could not fail?"

It's a powerful question.

I think it's also important to ask, "Why wait until you know you're dying to start living?"

Why is it that it takes some kind of horrible news for people to do things they've always wanted to do? People who know they will die in the not-so-distant future often talk about the fact that they've never felt more alive. Do you know why? They realize time is limited. They aren't waiting because they *can't* wait for the "right time" to come around. So, they just *do*.

They go skydiving. They tell someone they love them. They start dancing, or singing, or painting. They travel and befriend strangers. They try new foods and ride that scary roller coaster for the first time. They do the things they were afraid to do before. They forget about the option of failure or maybe, they just start looking at it a different way.

After all, failing doesn't make you a failure. But waiting to do something *does*.

Please understand that trying and failing aren't just for the young. They are for all of us. Some of the best failures come when we're old enough to understand that so-called "failing" simply means we found another way that something won't work. Failing at something means that we're alive and we tried.

I don't know about you, but I don't want to live my life afraid. And I do hope you find something relatable in this book that touches your life in a positive way. But if you don't, at least I finally wrote the book.

27

love is the thing

When I first saw Doug, he came around the corner of a building driving his bright yellow backhoe. I imagine that the majority of people in his life met him in a similar way. If he wasn't driving a backhoe, it was a trailer, a souped-up golf cart, his cooler-than-Elvis motorcycle with the sidecar, or some other impressive motorized vehicle. I was 27 years old when I met him and had just started Joy's House.

Doug came around the corner like a knight in shining armor riding that yellow horse to rescue us in a moment of construction need…and he never stopped. For nearly 20 years, we called on him for everything. From small jobs like moving dirt from one place to the next, moving people for our open house, moving snow, or smashing down the trash in the dumpster, to big jobs like digging a new basement, he showed up every time. He might not have necessarily been *on time*, but he always showed up.

We were special to him, but so was everyone else. He wasn't perfect, but he knew how to love people by being there for them in a thousand different ways. He had a habit of rescuing people, whether you had a broken-down car or a broken heart, he was your guy. He was the guy who shot off fireworks by the river on Independence Day purely for the enjoyment of others and he was always faithful to assist with moving days. His consistency, his dirty hands, wrinkles from years in the sun, and his sincere smile made everything feel okay.

During the last handful of years before he died, Doug and I had some of our best conversations. He was proud of his most recent choices in life–his job as a motorcade escort for funeral processions, his deep love for his girlfriend, Phyllis, and his dog, Josie. I was grateful that Doug let me into his life. I wasn't just that chick down the street who ran some not-for-profit organization, I was family. He and Phyllis even asked me to officiate their wedding ceremony.

Doug was admitted to the hospital and his prognosis looked so bad we thought it was going to be his last day of life. A bunch of us made our way in and out, some arrangements were made, beautiful things were said. I designed their marriage ceremony, just in case, because it seemed clear that Doug wasn't going to make it to August when he and Phyllis had planned to be married. But then, like a light switch, something changed early in the afternoon and his condition began to improve, at least for a few more days. We all gave hugs and kisses and made our way home, thankful for a little more time with Doug.

But pretty soon, Phyllis called and knew Doug's last day of life had arrived. She told me to hurry because he was transitioning. I got to the house as fast as I could. His family and dearest friends were there…preparing. I went to the bedroom to see him. When I walked in, his back was to the door, and I could see the outline of his spine through his clothing. He looked so small lying in the middle of that bed.

I moved around the bed so we could see each other's eyes, and said, "Hi." He mouthed the word back to me, saying more with his eyes than he could muster up with his voice. Phyllis gently placed herself next to him on the bed, cradling his body with hers. The three of us sat together for a moment in silence. Phyllis had placed a cross beside his head that I had given to him a week earlier at the hospital.

After clearing my throat, I practically whispered, "I'm so sorry that I never asked to pray with you."

Phyllis responded with confidence, "It's not too late." The three of us held hands, Doug's hand in ours, and we prayed. We prayed for love. We prayed for redemption. We prayed for transition and peace.

After the "amen" I looked at the two of them together and thought of their wedding day that would never arrive. Sitting next to this beautiful couple, knowing that the moments were slipping away, I realized that I still had their wedding ceremony written out in my car.

I took a moment outside on the front porch after grabbing the ceremony to pause, to ground myself, and I was quickly flooded with love and memories of this man who had rescued me, and countless others, so many times over the years. When I walked back inside, his room was filled with the people who loved Doug most. His mom and dad, sisters, and friends were gathered around his bed. Phyllis remained in her position, holding Doug comfortably in place, and Josie even put her paws up on her dad's legs as we began what was to become their wedding.

Drawing their attention to the cross, I asked that each person take a moment to hold it and pray for our beloved Doug. He was tired. He appeared ready to go, yet everything in him fought to stay with us for this moment in time.

I encouraged both Doug and Phyllis to look inside their hearts, to think about the life that had led them to this day. Then I asked them to stop and acknowledge that nothing compares to the love the two of them shared together.

"You are natural together," I told them. "You have a beautiful way of bringing out the best in each other. And, while I know this isn't how you imagined your wedding, this is the way it was always supposed to be. God had today planned for you all along."

The cross was handed back to Phyllis and she placed it in Doug's hand, then gently put her hand over his. I asked, "Do you, Phyllis, take Doug, to be your beloved spouse, knowing in your heart that you will be a faithful friend, and a loving companion all of your days and moments of life?"

She responded, "I do." I asked the same of Doug. We finished the ceremony, and I told them that this is the moment they would be pronounced as man and wife. The whispers of affirmation and love danced around the bed where they were lying curled up as one.

The expression on Doug's face calmed and his head relaxed deeper into the pillow. We all made our way out of the room, sharing *I love yous* as we found our way to the living room, leaving his bride, his mother, and his father to say their final goodbyes. Within minutes, he was gone.

I was honored to know Doug for two decades. There will never be any words to fully describe the privilege it was to be present with him right up to the very end of his life. And that commitment ceremony...I really think he was waiting for that. It was the love. It was the love of his family and friends as we witnessed these last few moments of his life. It was the love of his wife and the way she held him until the end.

It's been my privilege to be with a number of people at the end of their lives and, just like Doug, the *thing…the* thing that matters at the end of life seems to be love. Thankfully, it's also the one thing we can never run out of. It's said we have an endless supply and I plan to see if that's true.

28

you don't need proof to know who you are

Have you ever been to a powwow? Like a legit native powwow? If you haven't, you're missing out.

My great-grandfather was a French trapper living in Canada who married a local indigenous woman–a member of the Blackfoot tribe. I can only write that with semi-confidence because there isn't any official paperwork and I've also heard Shawnee, but Blackfoot makes the most sense based on the path of their migration to the United States through the Yellowstone area.

My great-grandmother died when my grandma was a young teenager. Grandma's dad, a fisherman, moved to the west coast of Washington state and raised his daughters there the best he could. The traditions and stories that would have been handed down by her mother faded with every passing year, but at her core, my grandmother had that Aboriginal spirit. She valued harmony and nature, honesty, and resilience. She loved animals, and she loved her tribe.

As a young girl, her dad ran across a seal pup on the shore while he was out fishing. Its mother was nowhere to be found and his two young daughters adopted the baby seal and raised it until it was old enough to live on its own. Throughout my life, I've heard about the baby seal adventures and I've even seen a picture of my grandmother walking along the beach carrying the seal pup in a backpack.

Grandma's father and sister both died when she was fairly young and after she married and had her children, she was drawn to her native roots. She gravitated toward Aboriginal attire and a tribal style of community. She valued caring for the earth and the relationship between people and our planet. Though she died when I was a teenager, I still clearly remember conversations with Grandma about spirituality and the attention she gave to anyone or anything in need.

My aunt felt it, too. I wasn't very old when my aunt introduced me to the Aboriginal community in my hometown. I remember being nervous before going to my first powwow, having no idea what to expect. I remember the drive there, windows down, wondering what these people would be like and whether or not they would welcome me into their group. We rounded the corner and pulled into the drive.

From the moment we arrived, I knew that these were my people. The smell of a bonfire filled the air. Kids were running around, laughing and playing. Ribbon decorations were everywhere. Women carried their babies in cloth wrapped around their bodies. And the entire atmosphere was an invitation that I willingly accepted.

The Turtle Clan was their name. At least that's the name I remember them by. They held meetings, dances, gatherings, and the occasional pow-wow. My first outfit was a brown dress with fringe and splashes of turquoise and white throughout that I'm pretty sure my aunt handmade herself. My official moccasins completed the look. Okay, they were actually Thunderbird Minnetonka moccasins, but they were awesome, and I could wear them with just about anything, even on a non-powwow day, because they rocked.

Our chief was Chief Spotted Deer. Our medicine man was named Shepshee...or Shipshey...or something like that. I was a little girl, so I may have said it wrong. But, man, he was cool. He was always in his *regalia*, which is the clothing or adornments that Native people wear during powwows or social dances.

My aunt tells a story about the time a small group from this clan was traveling and stopped to get something to eat. They were all wearing traditional clothing that gave a nod to their roots, but when Shepshee walked in, time stopped. Everyone stared. People whispered. Then the group was turned away. They had to work their way down the road to find a place that accepted them just as they were, feathers and all.

Years later, Shepshee officiated my aunt's wedding. He also performed the ceremony for my grandma and her second husband. Standing in Shepshee's backyard, I was in awe of the ceremonial traditions–ribbons tied to fence posts danced in the breeze around the couple, a wedding blanket was placed around their shoulders, and special wedding songs were performed.

These memories and family stories would forever mark my life as an Aboriginal descendant. That is until I took one of those DNA tests. Mine came back with 0.00% Aboriginal connections. I'm French and German. Throw in a little Irish. But Aboriginal? Nope. When I say that I was crushed, I mean… I. Was. Crushed.

My husband, a born and raised McIntosh, who knows his family crest and can trace back his people to a specific castle in Scotland. Even *that guy* has more Aboriginal blood running through his veins than I do.

Oh, it's a funny story for people to hear me tell at parties. But not fun for me to tell. I'm even getting worked up just typing this. Ha ha. Super funny, you guys.

Here is where I stop myself and make peace with something. No one can take away who I am.

I didn't have the privilege of knowing my great-grandparents personally. But I did know my grandma, and with full confidence, I can say that I am my grandmother's granddaughter. I value harmony and nature, honesty and resilience. I love my tribe. I love animals.

Those powwows were a part of my childhood, and those memories make me smile. And even if they weren't my people biologically, they will always be *my people*. They impacted who I am and how I relate to others by allowing me into their world, regardless of how young I was at the time or the small amount of time I spent with them. I'm sure (or at least I hope) my Northwestern European ancestors were wonderful humans. But I am convinced that I found my people. And I knew they were family the moment I walked in those moccasins.

I tell you this story to encourage you to find the people who remind you of who you are. Whether or not there's an official paper trail, or you can fully explain it on your Ancestry account, I want everyone to know the incredible feeling of being among people who make you feel connected to your truest self–people whose kindred spirits you can carry with you for the rest of your life.

29

give real hugs

There was a time in my life when I couldn't be hugged by the people I love because my body was weak, exhausted, and I was susceptible to illness. Chemo was hard for a lot of reasons, but not being able to hug was a big one. I'm a hugger. And it's no mistake that the word *embrace* found its way into the title of this book.

During chemo, I could go from being well to being exhausted and sick within a matter of minutes. So, I couldn't hug people who came to visit me. It was just too risky. I had to sit a short distance away from them and smile through a medical mask. But every time friends came or left, I wished I could just wrap my arms around each and every one of them.

Chemo ended, then in a matter of weeks, the pandemic hit. Suddenly we were *all* susceptible to illness. We were *all* exhausted. We were *all* wearing masks. We were *all* sitting a short distance away from others. We took our life into our hands just touching each other, much less hugging.

They (I don't know who *they* are either, but *they're* real) say that touch deprivation during the pandemic has had a negative impact on our overall health and wellbeing. *Duh!* In our adult day services, 70% of our Guests passed away during the height of the pandemic. Do you know why? Social isolation. Lack of community. Limited or non-existent touch from people living outside of their homes.

Do you remember that first hug on this side of the lockdowns? I'm not talking about the one where you gave someone a side hug while wearing a medical mask underneath your cloth mask and turned your head in the opposite direction when you touched.

I mean the real one. The one where you went in without hesitation and stayed for a moment longer than you normally would. That is what I'm talking about when I say a *real hug*.

Real hugs increase oxytocin in the body (which helps us overcome feelings of loneliness), raise serotonin levels (which elevates our sense of happiness), strengthen the immune system, improve our sense of trust, relax our muscles, and regulate the nervous system.

That all makes me want to hug you right now.

Because I'm a hugger, I notice if a hug doesn't feel quite huggy enough. Sometimes a half-hearted hug feels like a limp handshake–weak, insecure, and kind of insulting.

What does a *real* hug look like? Well, it's reported that it must last for at least twenty seconds to give us the full benefit. Are you thinking what I am thinking? Twenty seconds is a lonnnnnnnngggggg time.

Do me a favor. Stop reading and count to twenty–old-school seconds, my friend, like with *Mississippi* in between each number. Go ahead. I'll wait. One *Mississippi*. Two *Mississippi*...

Now, imagine being in my arms for that amount of time. (Yep, it just got a little weird for me, too.)

I made the mistake of telling my husband about this 20-second hug thing. Now, just when I think we are done with a pretty nice hug and start to pull away, I will hear him mutter, “Twelve, thirteen, fourteen…” I’m not sure if he is going for the benefits or if he’s just mocking me, but either way, I settle back in and accept it.

I wish I didn’t know what the world feels like without hugs, but I don’t want to live in that world again. And even if I don’t stay in a hug all the way to 19-*Mississippi*, 20…I can appreciate now, more than ever, the fact that a real hug is important for so many reasons.

Here’s the thing. If I am going to hug someone, I need us both to mean it. No limp handshake. A good, strong, face-to-face bear hug is something the world needs more of. Now more than ever.

30

know how to throw a ball

When my oldest daughter, Maia, was little, I made sure she learned how to throw a ball. Was this because I loved sports, especially softball, as a kid? Maybe. Was it because knowing how to throw a ball strengthens muscles and improves hand-eye coordination? It's possible. Did it have to do with the physics behind throwing a ball? Absolutely not.

It's because it's fun! If you can throw a ball, you're *in*. You can play catch with anyone, anywhere, even your best four-legged friend. You can make memories. These were the real reasons.

Lucky for me, softball became a love in Maia's life, too. I can't possibly count the number of hours our family has spent wrapped in blankets, curled up in folding chairs, dragging a collapsible red wagon, cheering on our pitcher, or center fielder, or whatever position necessary. Because our girl was a pretty darn good softball player. She was fast as could be. No one could catch her when she was running bases. She was also a really good pitcher. But to me, something about her playing center field was especially fun to watch.

When that ball would come her way, I absolutely loved watching her lock in on its location, charge the ball, scoop it up, hop, and throw... *Out!* Okay. She didn't throw someone out *every* time she got the ball. That would be ridiculous. But her games were a thrill.

Those were wonderful years. Our other two kids were raised on those softball fields and have their own memories of practices and games. But some of our most fun memories together weren't "official" games. They took place in the cul-de-sac where we lived when the kids were little.

At one time, there were somewhere around 15 kids living on that cul-de-sac. There were more kids than adults, by far. And among all the great times we had there–the trampolines, the dogs, movie nights, cookouts, scavenger hunts, birthday parties–a highlight was our pick-me-up ball games.

Sometimes we had real bases laid out. Other times pieces of cardboard or chalk marks served as our bases. Sometimes the teams were divided fairly. Other times it was kids versus adults, which seemed unfair, but not because we could hit better. We were at a disadvantage because our running speed left a *lot* to be desired.

I can't believe I'm saying this, but we never broke a window on a house or dented a car. That's really amazing, actually. We did bruise some egos and pulled a few hamstrings along the way. Minor damage in the scheme of things.

I'm sure my kids have regretted choices here and there during their lives, but learning to throw a ball is not one of them. Being on sports teams teaches a lot of good things, for sure. But those cul-de-sac ball games taught us the most important thing– that it was never about winning and losing. It was about the conversations that took place in between at-bats, it was the laughter we shared while we played so seriously yet looked so silly, and it was the relationships that developed.

What started with simply knowing how to throw a ball will never end, because we became part of each other's lives forever.

If you don't know how to throw a ball yet, it's not too late. You never know what will happen if you learn. I can tell you with complete confidence that you won't regret it. I predict that you might just connect with someone, or a whole gaggle of someones, in ways that wouldn't have been possible any other way.

31

it's okay to look over the edge

Journal Entry — September 16, 2019

I'm writing, knowing that no one is going to read this…yet. I want to capture my thoughts. I want to get into my own head. I want to be able to look back on this piece and see where I was before I found out what happens next with this diagnosis.

"It looks like it's cancer." I have been going to this wonderful oncologist for seven years because of my first diagnosis, but three days ago is the first time he's had to say those words to me because he isn't the doctor who had to tell me the first time. Hearing this from him was a shock. I asked some questions, we scheduled my next appointment, and we hung up the phone.

As I shared those same words with some of the people closest in my life, there were a lot of tears, but strangely, none of them have been mine. I have feelings, I swear, but they just aren't coming out as tears. Maybe it's because we have had to share these words with people four different times over the past seven years. Four times. My breast, Jeff's kidney, Jeff's Chronic Myeloid Leukemia, and now a new kind of breast cancer for me. It's ridiculous. It's like the worst game I've ever played and I can't even tell who is winning and who is losing since technically we're on the same team. It's almost embarrassing.

I don't blame people if they cry. I'm just not there right now. And I don't blame them if they brush it off like we just told them that we're passing a cold around the house or that I have a headache.

But it's not that simple. It's cancer.

Telling the kids was the thing I was dreading the most. They asked a lot of questions that we can't answer yet.

But when Georgia asked if this was the good kind or the bad kind, the answer was bad. Cancer isn't good. Ever. What she really wanted to know was if this is going to be the thing that kills me. And, like everything else, Jeff and I answered honestly.

"We don't know, Honey. It might be, but it might not be." I remember the first time I was diagnosed with cancer, I talked about allowing myself to look over the edge and see all of the scary things that might happen. When I look over right now, I see death. I just don't fear it. The week before I was diagnosed, I was feeling numb. I now realize that I'm not numb, I'm at peace.

If this is the thing that kills me, I want a few things.

I want Jeff to have permission to date and marry again when the timing is right for him. I want people to support him with that part of the journey. I want him to keep taking his inhibitor pill every night so that he can die of something other than cancer, like maybe some natural cause in old age like high cholesterol while riding his motorcycle through the countryside. That will mean that he dies super happy. I want him to remind our kids about not only the good things about me but my shortcomings as well. Our kids will need to know that I don't stand high on a pedestal and even though I can be alright, I have made a lot of mistakes in my life and have been so very far from perfect.

I want Maia to go to college and live her best life. I want her to make friendships that will last forever, and I want her to make great and silly memories along the way. I want her to use her skills for good and not evil because that girl has a lot of skills and some of them can go either way.

I want her to laugh a lot. I want her to fall in love and have pets and have classes that challenge her. I want her to know that she is, in fact, a lot like me and I am a lot like her. But she is her own person and will make her own way. It is going to be beautiful for everyone to witness.

For Web, I want him to continue to grow, knowing that he is smart and funny and worthy of the good things that will come his way in life. I want him to know that he's one of the most self-aware and empathetic people I know and that these qualities combined with his smile and genuine charm will serve him well throughout his lifetime. We told him about my diagnosis, and he said a lot of beautiful and touching things. After a moment of raw conversation in private, he said, "If you die, what are we going to eat?"

I laughed, but then realized he was serious. He asked me if I would make him a book of all of my recipes. He said it's not really as much about the food as it is about the memories that come with them. I told him that I can make that book, but that it would be even better if he and I started cooking together so that I can show him while I'm still here. He liked that idea. I do too.

Georgia. Don't try to hold her back because she has a force about her that can't be broken. I want Georgia to know that our family became complete the day that she was born. We felt it. Jeff got her a necklace etched with the quote, "Though she be but little, she is fierce!" from Shakespeare. So very true. Georgia is a light.

I want her to dance and sing, paint (maybe not the driveway and the basketball pole again), continue to be creative, and smile. Her smile is everything. When I was telling a friend about this recent diagnosis, Georgia chimed in and said, "Yeah, and I have acid reflux." There's that.

For all three of them, I want them to know that I'm sorry that cancer has been such a big part of their childhood. I hope that they can kiss cancer goodbye and never deal with it again in their lives. But I also want them to decide now what path they are going to take with it.

I want to challenge them… Are they going to be victims in their lives because their parents had cancer, or will they survive it? Can they use it as part of their stories, their testimonies? Can they be sad when their hearts tug at them, and then move through it to be an example to others who face adversity?

Because we all face adversity, and we choose if we are victims or survivors. I hope this is part of their stories of survival and strength, of family, community, and above all, faith.

Most of us aren't ready to step and look over the edge. But when that time comes, it's really okay. Letting myself do that allowed me to see what *might be* and yet, I had the comfort of knowing that I could just take a step back on steady ground and see things with more clarity.

32

leave situations graciously

If you and I were friends and you told me about an uncomfortable conversation you just had with someone, I would ask you how you left things. You might feel like you don't really care, but the reality is...you probably will at some point. Somehow, someday, the way you left that situation *will* come back around again, either in conversation, in your heart, or with that person. Maybe it will be at a college reunion, on vacation, in a board room...or in the bread aisle at the grocery store.

My friend Gabrielle dated a guy named Ty after college. The relationship was pretty casual, one that the kids nowadays would call "talking to," but not actually *talking* to. Anyway, it was casual. There were a fair number of dates. She met Ty's parents once when they were in town, they talked about where she was from, her job, what Ty was like as a little boy. They laughed and hugged when they left each other, but it wasn't like he had proposed marriage. I'm not sure he ever even called her his girlfriend to them, although he did slip and introduce her that way one night at a work party. Apparently, that got kind of awkward. Poor guy.

Ty seemed like a good person. He was kind. He was interesting. He was cute. Sort of fun. But it became pretty obvious to the rest of us that Ty needed to be kind, interesting, cute, and sort of fun with someone else. Gabrielle was clearly not into the relationship like he was.

Instead of being straightforward with him, she started pulling away. When he asked her if she wanted to go out to dinner, she made up excuses about not feeling well. Later he asked about a movie. She said she had a lot of work to do and couldn't talk for a couple of days. A walk next weekend? Washing her hair or some other lame excuse. She was blowing him off and everyone knew it except for Ty.

The poor guy kept calling. She kept not rcturning his calls.

Weeks went by and without any solution, his calls got fewer and fewer until he finally stopped calling altogether. Life went on.

Four months later. Gabrielle and I were at the grocery store gathering items to make soup and cheese toasties. (*Grilled cheese* for those of you who aren't from Ft. Wayne, Indiana. For those of us who are, they're *cheese toasties.*) Gabrielle took the shopping cart and went to get some good old-fashioned, not-good-for-you white bread, because *duh*. It's indisputably the best choice if you're making cheese toasties.

I was chasing down the cheese when I heard her coming up behind me whispering, "Ty's here! Oh my goodness. Ty is here. I never called him back. Hide me."

"It's okay," I said. "So you didn't call him back. It's really okay."

By this time, she was practically one with the end cap, peeking around like a spy. She mumbled some things about not calling him back…ever. Like many voicemails and texts left unreturned.

Oh, and the timing? She ghosted the guy right after meeting his parents. Okay, I was beginning to see her point and it kind of *wasn't* okay. That was also the moment when I realized we would be driving through Subway on the way home because we would not be sticking around long enough to get supplies for cheese toasties.

While I wasn't exactly proud of Gabrielle for the way she handled that, I get it. It isn't easy to have awkward conversations like the one she avoided with Ty. Every time I think of that night, watching this grown woman hide in the grocery store, I'm reminded of how much having that conversation would have paid off in the long run.

Thanks to Gabrielle and Ty, I have developed a simple test to help you know whether or not you've left an uncomfortable situation graciously. Ask yourself if you can run into the other person in the bread aisle at the grocery store and say hello. Could you look them in the eyes and wish them well? If not, maybe it's time to have that conversation. Giving someone closure, a simple explanation, or an apology is the gracious thing to do. And it is a whole lot better than hiding from someone for the rest of your natural life.

33

shake out the crabbies

"That's it," Jeff said from behind the wheel of our I'm-cool-in-spite-of-the-fact-that-I'm-driving-this mini-van. "Do we need to shake out the crabbies?!"

Growls and snide comments came from our three kids in the backseats. They knew he was serious, and they were getting to the ages when *shaking out the crabbies* wasn't as cute as it used to be. We had been doing this with the kids for as long as we could remember.

The concept is simple. Someone is in a bad mood. Their attitude is contagious and someone else becomes crabby. A pandemic is on the horizon.

Someone still has enough sense (thank goodness) to say, "Alright, everyone. Let's shake out the crabbies." With a cloud of disdain in the air, fists are formed but, somehow, like a miracle from God, we begrudgingly hold hands.

The wise person who has called this crabby-shaking counts, "One…two…three..." and begins to shake and rattle his or her or their body, which causes a small stir in the person whose hand they are holding. The leader pretends to spit out bad vibes and noises come from deep within that sound like a rafter full of wild turkeys, or maybe a litter of lonely puppies.

The rest of us in the circle feel the wave coming our way. We begin to make small noises at first. *Ugh. Grrrr.* A little rush of adrenaline is then released inside of us, and our arms begin to move. Then something strange happens to our mouths…a smirk… wait, that might actually be a smile. Yes! There it is! A smile!

Wise Person gives everyone a warm hug or a very dad-like fist bump, and we then go our own way, leaving the unwanted crabbies behind.

I don't know about you, but there are a whole lot of times when I just want to let myself be in a mood. I almost enjoy being mad in these moments, like I'm just hoping someone will come into the room and say something or look at me the wrong way. Please. Someone do it. Because I'm ready to unleash something bad, usually on someone good. (Not my best quality.)

On April 2, 2020, my journal captured one such day:

> Yesterday, I was crabby. After biting the heads off of my children, husband, mother-in-law, and the poor guy from the pest control company, I decided to let myself be crabby. Finally, I was able to say it. "I'm crabby because I'm afraid."

They all told me that they understand. Then Maia said, “Mom, it’s okay to *feel* that way, but you don’t get to push us away.”

Those. Are. The. Moments. *Those* are the moments I know we are doing okay as parents. I told her she was right and that I would find a different way for my emotions to show up, just to give me a little time to work through it.

“Okay, but if you don’t get through it soon, we might just have to shake out the crabbies,” my incredibly insightful daughter said in her best smart-aleck tone.

She was right. It's okay to be afraid. It's okay to feel any single emotion you need to feel. You do, however, have to make a conscious decision to keep the crabbies from taking over or you'll only isolate yourself and alienate the people who love you. Do whatever works. And if you've never tried shaking out the crabbies, you look pretty silly, it's worth a try and cheaper than therapy.

34

don't try to rationalize with an irrational person

To be rational means that someone is using reason. It means that they are fair-minded and usually open to listening to other perspectives. To be irrational is quite simply put…the opposite of that.

I've met a lot of irrational people in my life. Shoot, who am I kidding? I *am* the irrational person sometimes. Sometimes I'm irrational because I'm so angry I can't see straight and I start saying things I should not be *thinking*, much less saying out loud. Sometimes I'm irrational because I'm scared or frustrated. Instead of using my good words, I lose control and dig in my heels.

At Joy's House, irrational is our norm. It's not because our Guests don't *want* to be logical or reasonable. It's often because they *can't*. Each of them is living with some kind of diagnosis - Alzheimer's and other dementias, multiple sclerosis, strokes, traumatic brain injuries, Down syndrome, and other conditions that require safety, community, care, and purpose. Those are a few of the important things they get at Joy's House.

If a 96-year-old woman living with Alzheimer's disease tells me she wants to go home because her mom is making dinner, I'm not going to tell her that her mom died forty years ago. I'm going to ask her what she thinks her mom is making for dinner. We're going to talk about her favorite meals and the things that make her happy. No matter the diagnosis, people want to be happy and loved.

Mr. Rudy was happy. He sure was loved. He was one of my favorite irrational Guests of all time. He was an older man who had been a boxer all of his life–like an in-the-ring boxer. He was still in great physical shape, and I would have put my money on him in a heartbeat for a win should the gloves come off…or go on? I'm not sure how that saying really works.

Rudy looked fantastic in a fedora hat. He had a smile that I guarantee won the favor of many women throughout his life. He had been living with dementia for a number of years when he started coming to Joy's House.

He was always concerned about what time he was getting picked up and often suspicious about the people around him. Every day he made jokes, talked about boxing, and insisted that he had to go to the bank to *take care of his business.*

On one otherwise calm Tuesday afternoon, Mr. Rudy decided it was time to go to the bank. On this particular day, no one could tell him anything different and all of the attempts to engage him in an activity or conversation were failing.

"Lady, I have to get to the bank," he said calmly, and yet with some force, to my coworker, Theresa. Theresa was used to this and she used every trick she had in her bag.

"Mr. Rudy, your daughter will be here soon to get you." He took a step closer to the door.

"Mr. Rudy, it's okay. You don't need any money here. We've got you." Another step closer.

She attempted to redirect him over and over again. Every time, Mr. Rudy got closer to the door that would lead him outside, where he was convinced the bank would be waiting for him.

Here's the thing about a lot of people living with dementia–In their minds, what they are thinking and saying is real. Whoever is opposing them is the one who is confused or delusional.
Think about that for a moment. Think about a time when you knew, you just *knew*, you were right, and that other person was wrong. How do you know that *you* were the rational one in the conversation? How do you know it wasn't *you* who was delusional or irrational? In that confrontation, were you willing to argue for your win? Were you willing to fight for it?

Mr. Rudy was. He. Had. To. Get. To. The. Bank. And Theresa wasn't letting him. Often the person with dementia becomes paranoid or feels threatened and scared. Do *you* want to be the person who threatens or scares a lifelong boxer who must get to the bank *now*?

Well, Mr. Rudy made it out the door. (Don't ask. That's a different therapy session.)

Theresa had always had a great rapport with Mr. Rudy, so she casually walked outside to be with him and try to coax him back into the house. She was so casual that she had her coffee cup in her hand and took a sip every now and then.

When trying to communicate with an irrational person, if the person smells aggression, things can escalate quickly. It's critical to engage in a peaceful conversation, to validate what you're hearing, and to help redirect without any scent of aggression.

It appeared to Theresa that he was going to be easily redirected and would come back into the safety of Joy's House where all would be well again in our world. But Mr. Rudy had different plans. *He had to get to the bank.*

He took a step toward the side street. Then she took a step. He started walking faster, like he was just really trying to get in his Fitbit steps for the day. She started walking faster. Trotting was next, then a full-on chase across the street, down the sidewalk, toward a bank that didn't exist.

Things escalated so quickly that, by the time I got my eyes on them, they were exhausted. Both stood side-by-side, hands on their knees, panting. Mr. Rudy turned around, defeated, and started walking back to Joy's House. Theresa, hoping she could put this one down as a win, walked next to him. Next thing I knew, they were hand in hand. Which worked out, because Theresa's coffee mug was history after this sweet little footrace.

Soon I was able to greet them at the door, offer fresh cups of coffee, and make sure the door was secured behind them. Mr. Rudy smiled as he came in the room, looked around for a place to sit down and then paused. And you'll never believe what he said.

"Lady, I need to go to the bank."

He was ready for Round 2.

Someday, when you're looking into the eyes of someone who, for whatever reason, isn't able to think rationally, take it from Theresa and me, don't expect to rationalize with them.

35

time doesn't always heal

I recently got my seventh tattoo. It's on my left wrist and when I hold my hand palm up, I can see the outline of three birds sitting on a branch. They appear to be in conversation with each other and when I look at them, I imagine they're getting along and enjoying the view from the limb where they sit. They represent my three children.

On the outside of that same wrist, where I have to really twist and turn my arm to see them, there are three birds flying away. These three represent the babies Jeff and I lost.

Our first pregnancy brought us Maia. We were overjoyed to become parents and couldn't imagine our lives without her. We instantly knew love in a whole new way. Our lives had new meaning.

Our second pregnancy was ectopic. The baby was growing, but unfortunately, it was growing outside of where it was supposed to be. The option was to continue on with the pregnancy, where the baby and I would have surely both died, or we could choose to terminate the pregnancy. It felt like an impossible decision. And yet, I knew the answer. It was hard then and it's still hard for me to write the words. Jeff and I *had* to choose to end that pregnancy so that I could live.

Nowadays, people are told to wait longer than ten weeks after an ectopic pregnancy. But back then we were told that we could start trying to get pregnant in ten weeks. And since traces of the medication were still in my system, that baby didn't make it into the world either.

Webster was born the following year. He was the most beautiful baby I had ever seen and he was ours. Then I got pregnant again a couple of years later and there was a mass. In the battle of mass versus baby, the mass won.

Georgia was born a few years later and we knew then that our family was complete.

My kids were teenagers when I got that seventh tattoo. When the tattoo artist was done, he said, "Check it out. Let me know what you think."

I felt a lump in my throat. "It's perfect," I said, not looking at him and hoping he couldn't see the tears that kept filling my eyes. I was afraid that if I blinked, I might never stop crying. My last lost pregnancy happened nearly fifteen years earlier. Still, the tears came so easily.

I can't count the number of times people have said things like, "Just give it time," or "Time heals everything." I call BS.

I still think about those babies who never got the chance to meet their family. I think about all the love that would have certainly been showered on them, and

I think of everyone who would have gathered to celebrate their birthdays. I still wonder if they would have had Jeff's brown eyes or hazel eyes like mine. I wonder when they would have taken their first steps or if one of them–just one–might have said *mamma* before rattling off *dadda* after *dadda*. But mostly, I look forward to meeting them one day when my time is done on this earth.

I realize that if any one of those babies had made it into this world, I wouldn't have the family I have now. It didn't take long to understand that. And yet there is still a heartache, a pain that I feel when I think about those three little souls that I didn't get to meet. I remember how we felt each time I discovered that I was pregnant–elation, excitement, a fullness. Then each time we learned that the baby wouldn't make it, we felt deflated, alone, devastated.

We've given it time. Goodness, we've given it time. I don't think I'll ever be healed because time doesn't always heal. Time just makes things different.

36

have uncomfortable conversations over a meal

Years ago, I had to end a contract with someone from a consulting role in my organization. In short, she didn't fit our culture and I was getting too much negative feedback about her to continue trying to make it work. The time had come, and I had zero desire to have that conversation.

It would have been much easier for me to communicate through text or email. Heck, even calling her would have been okay, although you and I both know I would have been praying for her voicemail to pick up, so I didn't have to hear her reaction.

Instead, I forced myself to take her to lunch. I told her in advance that we were going to be removing her from the project, but I wanted to sit down and talk about it together. One of my goals at Joy's House is that I want every person who comes in contact with us to be better for the time we spent together and the experience of working together. In return, I want Joy's House to be better because of the individuals who have been part of making it what it has become and who the organization will be in the days ahead.

Veda and I met at a local restaurant. We sat in a booth, facing each other, waiting for our salads to arrive, making aimless small talk. Truth be told, it was hard, and I was nervous. But before too much time could go by, I asked what questions she had for me and I did my best to answer each of them.

At one point, I could tell that she was about to blow. She kind of leaned in toward me and in a disgusted tone said, "I know your type. You want to be friends with everyone."

I'm pretty sure that I lowered my eyes in thought and took a deep breath before saying, "That's not true. I don't want to have a friendship with everyone. I *do* want to have positive relationships with people I encounter on a regular basis, including you, and we're not there."

Her face changed and our conversation shifted entirely. We talked about what should happen next with our contract and how we could bring it to a quick close. She asked me what I suggested for some other work she had going on and I listened when she told me what she thought I could do better as a leader within my organization.

By the last bites of our salads, we were talking comfortably. We had acted like the adults we are and, although we weren't going to work together any longer, we were both better for the experience.

When we got up to leave, she thanked me for lunch, for the opportunity, and for the honest back-and-forth conversation. My personal and professional respect for her doubled over the course of that lunch.

I haven't seen her much over the years, but some time ago, I did hear from someone who knows her and she had given my name as a community resource to this man. In his words, "She told me that you would take excellent care of my family and me during his time."

When Joy's House started, I was 27 years old. I didn't know everything I needed to know. Shoot, I still don't know everything I need to know and I'm fifty. There have been people over the years that I wish I had invited to join me for a meal peppered with uncomfortable conversation because what we left with instead is much harder.

What situation isn't made immeasurably better by yummy food? I can't think of very many. And it definitely doesn't hurt to know you are surrounded by potential witnesses and a server who will be checking on you regularly to keep things from going too terribly off the rails.

This approach may not *always* be feasible. We probably cannot have every single uncomfortable conversation over a meal. But I've lost people that I really cared about because I didn't create the kind of setting where we could feel comfortable enough to *really* communicate, give and receive feedback, and ask questions. I wonder how those partings might have been different if I had invited them to lunch.

37

see yourself through someone else's eyes

Walker had heard people say things like, "Your dad has told me so much about you," plenty of times before. His usual answer was the typical and goofy, "Uh oh, I hope he told you the good stuff." Laugh. Laugh. But nothing would ever compare to the experience he had after his dad's surgery.

He got news that his dad had been rushed to the hospital right after his 4:00 pm class. He vaguely remembers throwing his clothes into a bag and rushing from his dorm to catch the train home. By the time he reached the hospital, his father was in recovery. Walker waited in the family waiting room with his mom and sister. It was strange because his dad had always been healthy and strong. No one saw this coming.

When the doctor came out to talk with them, it was getting late. She explained that everything had gone well, and that Mr. Chambers should recover just fine. Then she told them it would be best for them to come back in the morning because he wouldn't remember them being there anyway. So, they went home to a fatherless house and stayed up way too late reminiscing together.

The next morning, Walker was the last one up. His sister and mom had let him sleep in, and they went on to the hospital. He got ready quickly so he could join them. As he approached his dad's room, he overheard his voice but something about the way he spoke sounded different. Walker could tell his dad was talking to a stranger. He sounded a little more gruff than normal, which made sense because of the surgery. Yet, at the same time, his tone sounded softer.

"My wife told me that my youngest made it back to town last night."

Walker stopped just shy of the door.
"That boy is amazing, I tell you. He's in college, so I don't get to see him enough. Plus, I've always been kind of rough on him, you know? It's just how a father is. I see so much potential in him. He's smart and charismatic. A good-looking kid too. He takes after his father. What can I say?"

The woman laughed.

His father continued, "I remember when he was about 15, we were at a baseball game. I coached his team. I always coached. It drove him crazy, but it was my way of being close to him, of being close to his friends. He was having a rough game, but I wouldn't let up. He was so mad at me that I swear he would have thrown the ball at my head if I wasn't looking."

Walker could tell his dad was smiling by the sound of his voice.

"He got up to bat, two outs, a runner on first and third. Steve stole second thanks to Walker's conning, then *whap!* That ball sailed dead center. My kid could hit a ball but never like that. We ended up winning by one run. Walker's run. I like to take credit for that win. If he hadn't been mad at me, well, you know. I took the team out for pizza.

"At the end of the night, my boy came up to me and wrapped his arms around me. He didn't say a word. He just hugged me. It was one of those hugs that says *thank you* and *I love you all* at the same time. I almost cried in front of all of those kids. It's one of my favorite memories. Anyway, I can't wait to see him."

Walker was frozen. He kind of shook his head to come back to reality and then walked through the door.

"Walker!" His dad almost sang.

"Hey Dad," Walker said.

The nurse pivoted and started toward the door. "It's nice to meet you, Walker," she said. "Your dad has told me so much about you."

He nodded hello, smiled at her, and headed straight for his dad. As he got closer, he asked, "I'm not going to hurt you, am I?"

"Not a chance."

"Well then," he leaned in and embraced his dad.

Neither of them said a word because they didn't have to.

Wouldn't it be wonderful if everyone could see ourselves through the eyes of someone who loves us? Just imagine it…you would finally get to see how talented and smart, gorgeous and fun you are. Oh, it would be incredible!

And let's remember to tell people the good we see in them. Everyone is better off when they hear the good things they bring into our lives, the memories we most cherish with them, and the reasons we are proud of them. And let's not wait until we're lying in hospital beds to share these things with each other. Maybe the time is right to do it now. Or at least very soon.

38

accept a compliment

In a small village on the west coast of Michigan, September 8, 2001, Jeff and I got married. The festivities leading up to the wedding included a bonfire gathering, a golf outing, shopping, active participation in a rodeo, and bull riding. I mean, really…doesn't everyone ride a donkey and a mechanical bull the night before they get married?

Something I've learned about myself over time is that I don't really like to be the center of attention unless it's for someone else or a cause I believe in. Things like officiating someone's wedding or speaking at a gala for Joy's House appeal to me. But that entire weekend, Jeff and I were at the center of everything for good reason. Everyone was so excited for us and our days were full of compliments and excitement. It was wonderful and exhausting all at the same time.

On the day of our wedding, I spent the morning walking the beach with a few close girlfriends. We talked about our concern of rain (which went away), the realities of marriage (which are both great and challenging), and the beauty of being loved by nearly 150 people who had traveled for hours and poured themselves into this quaint space to celebrate us (so many, in fact, that we spilled into neighboring villages). In fairness, we thought maybe fifty people would attend, since it was a destination wedding of sorts. It wasn't like we chose to get married on the other side of the world. But still, attending did require some effort.

Once back at the house we had rented for the week, Jeff prepared for the ceremony in the basement, and I got ready upstairs. We vowed to not see each other until the wedding, so he left early for the ceremony site. When it was my turn, I took a big inhale, ready to walk into the next chapter of my life. We said a prayer, then we walked, and walked, and walked. No shoes, just me in my simple wedding dress, a couple of dear friends, and my dad, Tom who would walk me to the ceremony and then hand me off to my biological dad, Ken, to give me away.

The house we had chosen sat high on a steep bluff and the wedding site was located below on the beach of Lake Michigan. You had to walk through some greenery and over two small sand dunes on the way. Before you got there, though, you had to descend about 5,436,982 steps, covered in sand. Of course, there weren't actually 5,436,982 steps. I lost count, but it sure did feel like millions.

After walking for what felt like days, we heard someone yell at us. We looked around. Nothing but dunes and lots of sand at this point. Then we heard it again. I looked up to see two middle-aged couples standing at the top of a bluff on our left.

"You look beautiful!" yelled one of the women.

I stopped walking. "I couldn't hear you. What'd you say?"

"You look beautiful!" she repeated.

I smiled. "I actually heard you the first time," I yelled back, "I just wanted to hear you say it again!"

The next person to tell me I looked beautiful that day was my soon-to-be husband. I didn't make him say it twice, but I did grin when I said thank you. Then I married him so now he's stuck with me forever.

A wedding day is exceptional, I understand that, but hear me out on this one. If a random person told me I looked beautiful on any other day, my response would have been very different.

"Oh, thanks, um…I didn't really do anything to myself today."

Or…"You think so? Wow. I don't really like this outfit on me."

Any number of ridiculous responses would have come out of my mouth. But why? Why is it so hard to hear a compliment and accept it? Some people might say it's low self-esteem. Others may explain it as a way for people to avoid coming across as conceited.

Whatever the reason, I wish we could just learn to accept a compliment. Not only is it good for our self-esteem, but the smile or giggle a compliment often brings is said to reduce stress and release chemicals in our bodies that make us feel good from the inside out.

Do you know how easy it is to accept a compliment? It can be as easy as two words. Say them with me…
"Thank you."

Or you can go crazy and add four more. "I really appreciate that." Your choice.

If hearing it once isn't enough for you, just say, "I'm sorry, what did you say?" And they'll say it again! Trust me, it feels just as good the second time.

39

we all have scars

It was football season, and we went to a friend's house to watch the big game. There were trays of cheeses and veggies, buckets of beer, and buffalo cheese dip. (Ooh, I could tear up some buffalo cheese dip right now!) We were clearly with *our people*. Old friends and new bonded with every yard gained and celebrated each missed tackle as our team took one step closer to winning the title.

I could hear people talking about their dogs. One of them was not laughing as she shared that her little dog somehow knocked over the kitchen trash can right before she left that afternoon. Apparently, her living room carpet got completely destroyed. Others shared about their jobs. One was really happy because he had just closed a big account, and another said that he was thinking about leaving his company because he just didn't feel challenged anymore.

I found myself in the kitchen having a different kind of conversation with a man I had never met. His name is Scott. Scott had cancer. On his face. Under his eye, to be exact.

He had undergone surgery just 23 days earlier to remove a walnut-sized tumor resulting from an aggressive form of Squamish Cell Carcinoma. Unlike most cancers of this nature, Scott's radical form of skin cancer had grown from within, making his experience one in millions.

There he stood in our friend's kitchen, dressed in Colts' gear, a bottle of beer in hand, and he was wearing a beautiful scar across the right side of his face. That scar was fresh. It was still raised from the skin. It had a redness to it.

We talked about his diagnosis and treatment. We talked briefly about my cancer journey. We even managed to talk about our winning team. But when it was nearing time to go, I asked him if I could touch his scar.

It was an odd request. We all know I'm weird. I get that. But I wanted to touch it. I wanted him to know that I saw him and his scar and that it didn't scare me. He was cool with it. You see, life-threatening diagnoses have a way of opening us up to things we never understood before.

I reached out and touched his face. He kind of closed his eyes and leaned in a little.

He said, "No one has done that yet. As a matter of fact, a lot of people pretend they don't even see it."

"I see it. It's beautiful, Scott," I said. "I like your scar. It means you're still here. I'll be praying for you to kick this thing's ass."

He smiled and said, "Thank you," in a voice that told me that he would try.

Scott and I have run into each other a few times since that Sunday afternoon. It's usually been in passing when we have only enough time to hug, ask how the other is doing, and move along, but I keep up on his health through our mutual friend. I know he had a second round of this stupid cancer not too long ago.

When I realized that I wanted to write about him, sharing that day we met, I called him.

"Hey, Scott. It's Tina McIntosh," I said when he answered.

"Tina! Hi."

After spending a few minutes talking about health and families, I said, "This is going to be odd, but I want to talk with you about your scar. Would that be okay?"

He immediately said *yes* and we started talking further. I asked him if he remembered the first time we met the way that I do. He did and he went on to share something that nearly brought me to tears.

"When you asked to touch my scar, I remember thinking, 'She's not afraid of it.'"

He took a second. "'*I'm* kind of afraid of it, but she's not.' That really changed things for me."

"How do you feel about it now?" I asked with curiosity because it's been five years.

"It's like the tale of two identities. Part of me wonders, 'What in the world happened to me? Of all the places for a tumor to grow on my body, underneath my eye?' I can't hide it and that's sad to me. The scar has actually healed really well, but since they had to cut so much out, my face has a sunken look to it on one side. A void of sorts."

He paused, "On the other hand, it's my trophy. I conquered. I got through it. It's a reminder that this can happen to anyone. All I can do is get up tomorrow and take on another day."

I told him that I still think his face is beautiful and thanked him for talking with me. I could tell he was smiling when we said goodbye. Scott's comment about not being able to hide it kept my attention and got me thinking. We all have scars.

Every single one of us. I have scars, for sure. You have scars. It might be on your arm from that tree you used to climb. It might be on your head from that clumsy fall you had when you were a kid. Maybe it's on your stomach from that scary surgery so many years ago.

Or maybe, just maybe, that scar is on your heart from that time when your mom got so mad at you that you didn't know if you'd survive. Or when that guy broke your heart into a million pieces. You might wear yours on your face too.

Scars show us that we have been through something real. They signal that we're still here and that we got to the other side of something hard.

I'd like to suggest that we all stop trying to hide our scars and, instead, learn to let them tell the story of our strength. I suggest we realize that they are the trophies and that people we love want to celebrate with us, not run from them.

40

embrace the imbalance

Balance what you eat. Balance your relationships. Balance your schedule. Balance your work and personal life. Balance. Balance. Balance. Balance everything. All. The. Time.

I mean I get that if you're going to have a piece of cheesecake the size of a soccer ball, you probably need to pack in some spinach and salmon. I understand that if you've been working a ton and you're constantly on-the-go, you might want to slow down now and then. Maybe take some moments to meditate, read, or spend time with someone you love. But is that really *balance*?

Or is that *embracing the imbalance*? There's a substantial difference.

Balance is about keeping things symmetrical–identical on all sides. It's about things being equal. If we were told to draw a picture of balance, we'd probably draw scales and balance beams. Maybe we'd get creative and draw a ballerina or someone riding a bicycle. Oh, tightrope walker would be good. Can you imagine being a tightrope walker? Just one small mistake and down you go…spinning, confused, scared, weightless until you're not.

That's what trying to find balance in my life can feel like. Just one small mistake and down I go.

I don't like that feeling and for me, it's not the way I want to live. I erased my belief in balance as a guiding principle in my life a long time ago. I'm not a tightrope walker. Trying to balance everything all the time is simply not possible. And it's exhausting.

The more I tried to balance things, the more I felt like I was perpetually behind or somehow *less than*. I felt like I was letting myself, and everyone around me, down–like I wasn't good enough at, well…anything.

Do you know why? Because I'm not good at everything, especially all at once. There are days when I am a great wife and not so good in the office. There are other days when I don't spend as much time as I would like with my kids, but I rock a presentation. Sometimes I'm an incredible friend who shows up with old stories and new memories and sometimes I fall really short as a friend and don't reach out for weeks or months or longer.

There is something that I value way more than balance. It's being present. Like *really* present, wherever I am. I want to be great *right here*. And when this time is done, I want to move on and be great for the next person, the next moment, the next thing.

Giving yourself permission to embrace the imbalance in life isn't about taking anything away. On the contrary, it's giving you permission to shine right where you are. *Be great right here.*

As you turn the page to move on to the next thing in your life, I hope you show up as the best version of yourself because you, my friend, were made to do great things. You were born to fill this beautiful and confusing world that we live in with love and care.

The next time you find yourself trying to do all of the things and you feel like you might be falling short, I encourage you to stop for a moment. That might just be the perfect time for you to embrace the imbalance and to be really great right where you are.

USA TODAY's Women of the Year honoree from Indiana 2023, Tina McIntosh is an entrepreneur, author, and speaker. She is the founder of Joy's House, a national-award-winning adult day service in Indianapolis, Indiana, specializing in caregiver support and education.

She is also a breast cancer survivor, the wife of a cancer survivor, mom to three remarkable humans, and co-host of the Caregiver Crossing radio show for family caregivers. She inspires audiences of all sizes on topics such as choosing joy, living your dreams while staying true to your core values, and embracing the imbalance.

Connect with Tina at embracetheimbalance.com or email tina@embracetheimbalance.com regarding speaking engagements, interviews, or appearances.

Printed in the USA
CPSIA information can be obtained
at www.ICGtesting.com
JSHW012258070823
46067JS00008B/23

9 798218 177133